WALKS THROUGH HISTORY
LIVERPOOL

WALKS THROUGH HISTORY
LIVERPOOL

DAVID LEWIS

The City of Liverpool

First published in Great Britain in 2004 by
The Breedon Books Publishing Company Limited
Breedon House, 3 The Parker Centre,
Derby, DE21 4SZ.

To Sean Halligan and Jeff Young,
my walking fellows.

ISBN 1 85983 403 9

Printed and bound by Scotprint, Haddington, Scotland.

Contents

Liverpool Record Office

The City of Liverpool

LIVERPOOL
the world in one city

Liverpool Record Office collects, preserves and makes available archives and local studies material relating to all aspects of the history of the city and its inhabitants.

You can find out about your family history, the history of your house, Street and district, famous Liverpool people and landmarks, and much more.

Extensive collections are held dating from the 13th century to the present, some of which are of national and even international significance. They include archives of the City Council and its predecessors, churches, cemeteries, schools, workhouses, families, businesses, trade unions, charities and societies.

Liverpool Record Office is run in conjunction with the Local Studies Library and Merseyside Record Office. This means that there are many collections all available in one place. There is also a major reference and lending library in the same building. The Local Studies Library has thousands of books, street and trade directories from 1766 to 1970, electoral or voters' registers from 1832—1914, 1918—1939 and *1945* onwards, and copies of many local newspapers from 1756 to the present day. There is a large number of street maps and Ordnance Survey maps.

There are significant collections of photographs from the late 19th century onwards. Some of these have been digitised. There is also a fine collection of over 5,000 watercolours.

There are copies of the census returns for Liverpool and the surrounding area and the Wirral from 1841 to 1901, national probate indexes from 1858 to 1951, and copies of the births, marriages and deaths indexes for England and Wales from 1837 to 2000.

We have a range of publications. These include leaflets and lists on many key sources for family and local history. There are also local history books, reproduction maps, and a CD-ROM containing *650* archive photographs and film footage.

We are leading a project for a major digitised history of the Port of Liverpool, its people and the surrounding area at http://www.mersey-gateway.org. This will include 20,000 images.

We welcome the offer of material for safekeeping by deposit or donation.

Liverpool Record Office, Central Library, William Brown Street, Liverpool L3 8EW
Tel: 0151 233 5817/5811
Fax: (for Central Library) 0151 233 5886
Email: RecOffice.central.Iibrary@liverpool.gov.uk
Website: www.liverpool.gov.uk

Appointments are essential for consulting some sources — please check before visiting.

Introduction

City walking

The best way to explore a city is on foot and walking the city's streets can be as rewarding and interesting – and invigorating – as a stroll in the country. We see sunlight and shadow on great buildings and not a distant mountainside, but the sense of exploration and discovery is the same, the discovery of unknown streets, buildings, even pubs or bookshops. There is poetry on city streets; the poetry of brick and soot, concrete and sunlight, street names and unexpected views. City walking enables us to explore a landscape at a slow pace, to double back and revisit, to vary the pace of exploration. It shows us the city's tiny treasures, the granite kerbstones or stone flags, the manhole covers, the ornate iron grilles, and allows us to sit for an hour with a coffee and watch the street.

City walking is about learning to observe and perhaps record city life, to examine buildings, rooflines and street surfaces (or 'footscapes') and to begin to understand what we like about the city and what we don't. All cities have a palimpsest quality, a quality of an erased and reused manuscript, streets demolished and rebuilt and then cleared again. Layers of history are uncovered as the eye is drawn to details of brick and stone, ironwork or roofline, to streets that work and streets that don't. How can a street not work? It is possible for streets not to work on a human scale, for them to be dreary canyons between shops or built merely for vehicles. The city walker sees the city differently from the office worker or someone running for a bus; they have the time to step back and *absorb* city life, to explore a building, a street or a landscape in some detail.

Liverpool

It has recently been announced that the city will be the European Capital of Culture for 2008. For the city council and property developers, this news was greeted with unrestrained joy. But for people who have been involved with the city's culture for some time – and have weathered the apathy and indifference of the council in the past – the news was greeted with some scepticism, as it is feared that much of the genuine character and culture of the city will be sacrificed for short-term gain. Yet many commentators wrote that the title is not a reward for what has already been achieved, but the shot signalling the start of regeneration on a previously unimagined scale.

In comparison with other cities Liverpool has vast tracts of land with no value, and probably has more unused land in the city centre than any other British city. Over half a century since the end of World War Two, Liverpool still has bombsites and the city walker will all too often come across the sites of lost buildings, some of which are ruins, some of which are holes in the ground. But how much of this will be changed in the next four years remains to be seen.

What is clear is that by 2008 Liverpool could be a very different city from the port that has been losing population and struggling to find a role since 1945. Now is a good time to explore the city as it is, and begin to mark the changes that will culminate in the city's 800th birthday in 2007 and the Capital of Culture celebrations the following year. After that, the city will supposedly be unrecognisable.

Drawings from earlier regeneration strategies in the 1970s show people standing on clean streets in warm sunshine, gazing at shiny glass and steel buildings, into a future that is warm and Mediterranean and free of many of the ordinary things of city life; traffic, rain, crowds. It will still rain in Liverpool after 2008 and the streets will still be occasionally dirty; there will probably still be graffiti and litter. But perhaps the city looks its best in the rain, and perhaps the changing light and weather add subtle, muddy colours to the palette of city life. The city will always be a mixture of old and new, dark and light, and only walking the streets can show us the city in all its moods and splendour.

Liverpool walking

This is a book of walks through the history of Liverpool, but it is also a book of impressions of the landscape of the city, and any history or stories are intended to give background and depth to those landscapes. The walks in this book reflect different interests in the city; there are family walks or shorter walks suitable for a gentle afternoon with children, historical walks exploring a district of the city, and hardcore urban exploration walks for the dedicated enthusiast only. These walks pass through the big tourist attractions but also explore the hidden city, a Liverpool of public gardens and elegant urban squares, of old men's pubs, quiet art galleries, and wide Georgian streets.

Clothing

In the city you are very unlikely to be as exposed as you would be on a hill walk, but some basic rules of clothing still apply. Wear sensible shoes or walking boots, have a waterproof coat and hat in your rucksack, and wear layers rather than heavy clothes. A rucksack is a good idea – it hides your camera, phone, notebook, maps, etc, and is a good repository for the acquisitions – the bus tickets, beer mats, second-hand books, pens, found objects – that city walking seems to attract.

Maps

You will not need a compass, but all these walks will be enriched by carrying the Liverpool A-Z and perhaps an old map of the area, such as the reprinted Ordnance Survey maps from the early 20th century. These will help you see the street in a broader context, to see how it fits in to the rest of the city, and also help trace vanished buildings or streets. A plastic folder is useful for when it rains.

Refreshment stops and transport

Most of these walks are suitable for a reasonably healthy adult, and some have been planned with children or younger people in mind. Refreshment stops and toilets are mentioned in the text, along with good pubs and cafés.

Security

Liverpool has a very low incidence of street crime, but just as rural walking demands a certain amount of common sense from the walkers, so does urban walking. I have only ever met curiosity and interest while walking the roughest areas of the city (usually from young lads – including one group who were building an igloo and one who were fascinated by the map of their street in 1908), but street crime cannot be ignored, so use common sense. You are probably safer walking in a group or in pairs; if you choose to walk alone, make sure that someone knows where you are; keep your eyes open and be 'streetwise', carry a mobile phone, and be sensible. Don't wave your camera around, keep phones or wallets out of sight, and keep an eye on who is around you. All cities have an equal measure of beauty and danger, and the remote chance of being the victim of crime should not stop us exploring them.

Thanks

Thanks are due to the following people, all of whom helped with this book; Eddie Calvert, Pauline and Dave Easby, Bill Harry, Charlie Keoghan, Dorothy and Reg Lewis, Jim Nolan, Stan Roberts, George Thompson, Simon Wilson. And a very big thank you to Justine Cook, who was endlessly patient with me when I had lost my sense of direction.

The Old Seven Streets

'...the past pervades the curious imperial quality of the city...'
Nicholas Wollaston, essay on Liverpool.

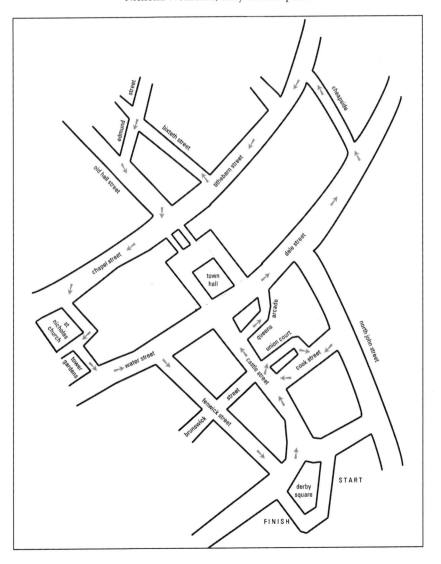

This is a walk around the oldest streets of Liverpool, which were possibly laid out by King John's engineers not long after the founding of the borough in 1207. It is impossible to say what was here before that date, although Roman and Saxon coins have been found in what would become the city centre. Cities destroy the past to build the future, and nothing survives of the mediaeval lanes or alleyways, the old wooden houses, the wooden wharves and quays. Instead this is the city's business district, wide streets of banks, shipping companies, insurance offices and hundreds of small businesses. The decline of Liverpool after 1945 meant that the old buildings were not demolished and replaced by faceless towers of glass and steel, and this is a landscape of Victorian office buildings, street after street of dynamic, eclectic architecture. Almost every side street and alleyway has something of interest; old-fashioned pubs full of smoky pin-striped meetings, busy cafés or coffee shops, ancient businesses in tiny cellars.

The first inhabitants were attracted to Liverpool by the opportunity of obtaining a 'burgage', which gave them certain rights and exemptions from some taxes and obligations. It has been estimated that the first settlers may have numbered as few as 150 families, and these 'burgesses' would have had houses fronting the narrow lanes of Castle Street and Dale Street, with vegetable gardens behind them, and further strips of land in the fields around. Covent Garden, which runs from Chapel Street to Water Street, was not originally named after the famous London district: rather it is a corruption of Common Gardens, a piece of land parcelled out in allotments, a remnant perhaps of common land right in the centre of the old town. The uncultivated lands around the small town were useful for grazing animals and for gathering fuel.

At the start of the walk, in what is now **Derby Square**, stood Liverpool Castle, the

Derby Square, 2004.

most important building in mediaeval Liverpool. It was built in approximately 1235 to guard the little town and port, and perhaps to garrison soldiers on their way to Ireland. There is nothing above ground of the heavy towers and high walls, but the Castle's moat was cut into solid rock and has been rediscovered many times by building work and sewage workers. The Castle stood on a headland, since what is now Paradise Street and Whitechapel was the original Pool, a tidal creek that ran as far inland as the Old Haymarket at the foot of St John's Gardens.

The Castle survived for approximately 500 years, and was only fully cleared in the middle years of the 18th century. The tall and elegant Baroque church of St George was built on the site, and regrettably demolished at the end of the 1800s after falling out of favour. Derby Square today is dominated by the Queen Elizabeth II Law Courts, which have something of the grim purpose and appearance of the Castle, with sandstone-coloured walls, formidable towers and narrow windows.

Perhaps because of this imposing presence, Derby Square is a bleak space. It has lost the bustle and life it had when the buses and trams ran from here, and the only people seem to be scurrying to the new castle to work in the courts; a stream of lawyers and clerks, witnesses and anxious families. The new office buildings thrown up in the 1960s are unattractive, and would be better demolished. It is difficult to avoid thinking that in France or Italy Derby Square would be crammed with little cafés and tables, for it is a sunny place and big enough to take a few café-bars.

Today the focus of the square at ground level is the Queen Victoria Monument, completed in 1905 and designed by F.M. Simpson, Professor of Architecture at Liverpool University. It was reviled and mocked for its conservatism and ugliness, but it appears tasteful and even elegant against the dirty concrete and glass around it. The bronze sculptures are by Charles Allen, who was Vice-Principal of the School of Art, and represent Agriculture, Commerce, Education and Industry, staunch Edwardian values. But famously, from one angle, Her Majesty appears to have a flaccid penis poking from the folds of her dress.

Castle Street is the heart of Liverpool's business district and from the Castle to the Town Hall is an almost intact Victorian commercial street frontage. Many of the buildings were originally banks, shipping offices or insurers and they were built to impress clients with their solidity and style. They are rich in carving and mosaic, a jumble of architectural patterns and styles, with a roofline tumbling with sculpture and domes, statues and ornate chimney pots. Nowhere else in the city is there this richness and variety of buildings. There are some modern additions, false teeth to replace a building lost in the Blitz, but these are usually quiet and restrained, as if realising that they cannot compete with the surrounding Victorian exuberance.

Some buildings stand out from the impressive crowd. The Trials Hotel opposite Derby Square was built in 1868 and was occupied by various banking companies for many years. It is an ornate building in yellow sandstone, heavily and massively decorated. On the corner of Brunswick Street is a coffee shop housed in the old Adelphi Bank. This is a humorous and flamboyant building, rich in detail of bronze and sandstone and polished

The old Adelphi Bank, Castle Street.

Charles Cockerell's Bank of England building, on the corner of Cook Street.

granite. Its swirling onion domes (and the ornate wedding cake statuary on the building next door) are a strong feature of the skyline. The architect, W.D. Caroe, also designed the equally unusual Swedish Seamen's Church on Park Lane. From the coffee shop can be seen the equally imposing Bank of Scotland building on the opposite corner. This was designed by Grayson & Ould and is a solid and intelligent building, with Liver bird and nautical motifs and a delicate turret emphasising the corner of Brunswick Street.

On the corner of Cook Street is a gigantic sandstone temple, built as a branch of the Bank of England between 1845 and 1848 by the great Charles Cockerell, who also worked on St George's Hall. The scale of the building makes it look bigger and more imposing than it really is, as it is only a little taller than neighbouring buildings. The old bank building is a very imposing terminus to Brunswick Street, and has been described as Cockerell's best work. The little **Union Court** behind is a glimpse of Dickensian Liverpool, probably named for the Union with Ireland in 1800. It is especially attractive at the weekend when the buildings and cobbles are not obscured by cars.

Cockerell's original design had further buildings behind the bank, facing onto **Cook Street**. The street was heavily bombed and Cockerell's extension destroyed, but the bombs missed the greatest treasure on the street, Peter Ellis's astonishing glass wall at 16 Cook Street. Ellis was a great architect whose buildings were ahead of their time, because of his use of technology and materials and his 'stripped aesthetic.' Only two of his buildings were ever built, both of them in Liverpool, and we will see his more famous Oriel Chambers later in the walk. No.16 Cook Street was built in 1866. It has the shape of a Victorian office/warehouse, but

The Town Hall
decorated for
Queen Victoria's
jubilee, 1897.
(LCC)

seems to be made of glass, with only thin ribbons of stone holding it together. At the crossroads below, Cook Street crosses North John Street to become Victoria Street, and gives a good view through the top end of the city to the cultural forum of buildings on William Brown Street. Century Buildings opposite has a frieze of playful cherubs and melancholy Art Nouveau maidens romping across it holding a ruffled sandstone nameplate – and was built nearly 40 years after Peter Ellis's building on Cook Street. Returning to **Castle Street**, we can see the imposing side of Cockerell's building, with its large windows allowing light into the central banking hall.

There is still a reminder of mediaeval Liverpool among the splendid commercial buildings on Castle Street. In front of the NatWest Bank is the Sanctuary Stone, one of two that used to mark the boundaries of the old Liverpool Fair, which was held on 25 July and 11 November. For 10 days either side of these dates the land between the Stones gave protection from arrest for those supposedly engaged in Fair business, a practice that continued theoretically until the Municipal Reform Act of 1832. The other Stone stood on Dale Street, near the top of Stanley Street, but no record survives of what it looked like and it has long since disappeared.

The imposing classical building facing Castle Street is Liverpool Town Hall, opened in 1754 and listed Grade I. The original building was designed by John Wood of Bath (who intended the ground floor to be used as a business exchange with the upper floors being used for municipal purposes) but it has been altered many times since it opened. It was damaged by fire in 1795 and James Wyatt was commissioned to reconstruct it. He added the imposing dome and, later, the Corinthian portico. Liverpool was not then ashamed of its trading links with Africa, and the frieze is decorated with the heads of African princes, unlikely camels and elephants. The interior work was not finished until 1820, but left Liverpool with one of the finest suites of civic rooms in the country. The building has a sooty Georgian dignity and the chandeliers, seen lit at dusk from Castle Street, are very beautiful.

Queens Arcade, opposite the Sanctuary Stone, is a narrow pedestrian way lined with small shops and coffee bars. It seems that it is built of pale golden sandstone, and is a useful short cut to the rush and tumble of **Dale Street**, the second of the seven streets.

To the walker, Dale Street is mainly seen on ground level or from across the road as it is always very busy with traffic. It is a street of large Victorian commercial buildings, but it also has a number of narrow lanes leading off into the wasteland of Moorfields, mainly used by office workers to walk from their cars to Dale Street, and there are many curious things and oddities on the street as well: humorous details and overlooked sculpture. It is a street to be admired or explored slowly, but again a few landmark buildings stand out.

Next to the classical Queen Insurance building we have just emerged from (with its fantastic royal coat of arms on the skyline) is the swirling magical Gothic of the State Insurance Building, truncated but the more fantastical for it. It was designed by W. Aubrey Thomas, who also designed the Royal Liver Building, although the two buildings could not be more different. This has large windows, a sci-fi Gothic glass tower, and stretched dynamic lines; it is playful and delicate, almost whimsical. The nightclub behind the façade was very fashionable during the 1980s.

The bank building on the corner of High Street opposite was built by Charles Cockerell and his son between 1855 and 1857. It is a classical structure in soft yellow sandstone, with unusual windows and a giant festooned doorframe, understated yet

Queens Arcade.

The coat of arms on the Queen Insurance building.

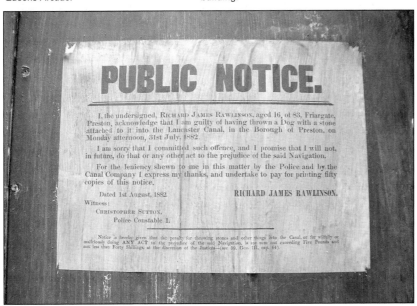

Fake notices on Sweeting Street, used as a film or TV set.

Gate on Sweeting Street.

Charles Cockerell's Liverpool & London & Globe building, viewed from High Street.

imposing. There is a story that when the site was cleared for this building the public liked the unexpected view of the Town Hall so much that an attempt was made to buy the land and keep the view, but nothing came of it.

The most imposing building at this end of Dale Street is the Royal Insurance Building on the corner of North John Street. Designed by J. Francis Doyle and opened in 1903, the building is draped around an unusual steel skeleton, in order to make the ground floor rooms as open as possible. It has elegant and chaste sculpture by Charles Allen, whose work we have already seen on the Queen Victoria Monument. Towards the roofline this giant stone building has the slightly surreal Baroque mood of the Port of Liverpool

The Royal Insurance building.

The Temple building, designed by James Picton, and the Royal Insurance building.

Building at the Pier Head. There are empty turret rooms, giant urns with lids like stone torches permanently ablaze and frozen, and deep arches of oversized stones. The Royal Insurance Company moved out some time ago and this splendid building, whose golden dome is a city landmark, is currently empty. The elegant Temple building next door was designed by the architect and writer James Picton in 1864 and has recently been renovated as offices for a law firm. He also built No.11 Dale Street, once the home of the Union Marine Insurance Company, and now modern apartments.

The more you look at the Royal Insurance building the more there seems to see, which is also true of Alfred Waterhouse's huge Prudential Assurance building further along the street, in the hard red brick and terracotta that he favoured. There is a figure of Prudence in

Architectural details on Dale Street.

the white stone doorway to Waterhouse's giant building, the defiant red brick and chunky tower of which make it a commanding presence on the street. A riot of Art Nouveau cherubs romp happily across the entrance of the Guardian Assurance Buildings opposite, playing instruments and wielding torches as if to disturb the office workers inside.

Municipal Buildings, built in the 1860s in a colourful jumble of architectural styles, is by far the dominant building on Dale Street. The tower and spire are another of the city's landmarks, and the building is powerful and dramatic, if unsettling to architectural purists. The building is open and accessible to the public, many visiting it to pay their taxes. Modern ironwork has enhanced the building's look, as has the retention of the lamps on the balustrade. The old Conservative Club across Sir Thomas Street is currently empty, but it too is pleasantly eclectic, with stone beasts roaring impotently from heavy carved foliage.

Trams on Dale Street, 1947. *(LCC)*

So far, Dale Street has been a parade of Victorian commercial grandeur. But the street is much older than this, and the small empty block opposite Municipal Buildings has a waterhead dated 1819. The narrow road beside it is **Cheapside**, one of the oldest roads in the city. It was originally called Dig or Duck Lane and was at one time the only lane connecting Dale Street and Tithebarn Street. The west side was built up before the mid-1700s, when the east side was partly gardens and partly tanners' and skinners' yards. The last of these disappeared when the police station was built.

This is still the city's main Bridewell, and presents a suitably grim, classical face to the

The Bridewell.

street. Brendan Behan was briefly incarcerated here in the 1940s, and the pub opposite is probably the safest pub in the city. There is an interesting, and almost intact, old shop frontage a little further on from the pub, and some tall and unobtrusive warehouses, but the top of the street has been built up with new buildings. They house students and car parks, and alone at the top stands the sadly missed United Powers pub, one of the few Georgian buildings in this area to survive, and recently blown up for the sake of a television play.

Turning left at the top of Cheapside leads us on to

A shopfront mosaic on Cheapside.

Tithebarn Street in 1915. *(LCC)*

Tithebarn Street, the third of the original seven streets of Liverpool. There were a number of barns on the street over the centuries, and the Tithe Barn itself supposedly stood close to the junction of Marybone and Great Crosshall Street, at the crossroads to the right. The original tithe barn was erected by the Molyneux family during the reign of Henry VIII and demolished before 1674. For nearly 600 years after the founding of the borough, Tithebarn Street was the last road to the north-west of the city. The street itself was described by Picton in its 'primitive condition' as 'tortuous, ill-built and narrow' and in parts no more than 15 feet wide. The Pall Mall side of the street was only built up in the 18th century and Tithebarn Street itself was widened in 1820, when any surviving mediaeval farm buildings were swept away. There are some Victorian survivors, most notably the old Bradford Hotel on the corner of Pall Mall, recently rebuilt after gutting by fire as offices for the Merseytravel Company. This end of the street is dominated by student accommodation, student pubs and college buildings for the John Moores University, a major force for regeneration in the city.

Yet for such an important and central city street, Tithebarn Street has been overlooked by developers. The pattern of narrow streets in Moorfields, between Tithebarn Street and Dale Street, has not been renovated since being cleared 30 years ago and is now serving as one huge car park. The city's back streets are very important for the character of Liverpool, and it is a black mark against the city authorities that this area is not put to better use. The old street pattern could be rebuilt with housing (for young and old, rich and poor) shops, bars, restaurants, perhaps art galleries and small squares or even tiny

Exchange Station seen from Moorfields, 1954. *(LCC)*

parks; it is this variety that makes many European cities dynamic and exciting. The cars could be parked underground or hidden in low-rise multi-storey car parks like Queen Square, cleverly designed to resemble the city's Victorian warehouses. But perhaps things are changing; the city block fronting Tithebarn Street is being developed again, and a new law centre is being built on empty ground opposite the station.

Exchange Station was built in 1886 by the Lancashire & Yorkshire Railway Company which ran trains from here to the north country and Scotland. Siegfried Sassoon, the writer most famous for his World War One poetry, always chose to stay in the station hotel when he visited Liverpool. It closed in the 1970s and was redeveloped as offices named Mercury Court, but the façade was retained and cleaned, and it looks very handsome from the two railway pubs opposite. On summer evenings the windows of the Lion in particular seem filled with creamy, golden stone. The railway lines behind the station have been transformed into a rather bland garden space and a huge car park. The original station, built in 1850 for the Liverpool & Bury Railway, was an elegant classical building like a country house, and was painted by Herdman in the 1860s. The 18th-century streets behind were gradually cleared as the station expanded, and among these the early home of the painter George Stubbs was demolished.

Turning right down **Bixteth Street**, we pass back into the Victorian commercial district, where an increasing number of large palazzo-style warehouses are being converted into luxury apartments. The warehouse on the corner of Ormond Street is an especially fine building, a Venetian Gothic warehouse with sleepy curled gargoyles guarding the ground floor. Bixteth Street leads to St Paul's Square, one of the quiet, dead places of the city. The area was known as Dog Field in the early 1700s, but became built up with fashionable houses later in the century, when the grand St Paul's Church was built. The area became more industrial, with warehouses and offices being built first for the Leeds & Liverpool Canal and later for the railway. All has gone; even the Liverpool Stadium which replaced the church has been demolished and the square now has nothing but the Cross Keys pub, popular at lunchtimes with local office workers, which retains much of its elegant 1930s modernity.

These narrow streets are quiet and relatively unexplored, and **Edmund Street** to the left is surprisingly tree-lined. On the left side is the massive Cotton Exchange, notable for its cast-iron panels decorated with elegant wreaths. Opposite is Stanley Hall, an exuberant Art Deco office building with giant and highly polished brass and bronze doors. The classical frieze on the inside staircase recalls the building's origin as offices for Silcock's, a firm of grain merchants.

At the end of the street is **Old Hall Street**, another of the original seven streets. The More family, important landowners in Liverpool for over four centuries, built More Hall in about 1230 on what is now the corner of Old Hall Street and Union Street, facing Edmund Street; only after they built a newer hall in Kirkdale was it known as 'the old hall.' In its prime the grounds of the hall stretched down to the river, and it was occupied until the early 19th century, when it was finally demolished.

The ancient fortifications of Liverpool crossed Old Hall Street. These earthworks were built of mud and brick, with a deep ditch beyond, and had 'mudwall' forts dotted along them. They were last used during the Civil War, when they were restored and possibly linked to one of the small forts on the waterfront. The Old Hall itself stood beyond the wall and suffered accordingly when Prince Rupert's Royalist troops laid siege to the town in 1644. The barns and outhouses were burned and the Old Hall itself was ransacked. The Royalists entered Liverpool along Old Hall Street, possibly after somebody had treacherously demolished part of the wall, and killed many people between here and the High Cross in front of the Town Hall, where the town officially surrendered.

Nothing survives of this ancient road. It was built up from the mid-1700s with warehouses and offices, but many of the later Victorian offices have survived and are now being redeveloped as restaurants, bars or apartments. Liverpool's newspapers, the *Daily Post* and the *Liverpool Echo*, are now housed in a huge office block on Old Hall Street, with a vast glass entrance hall big enough for a café and exhibition space. It is not an attractive building, but is certainly a landmark. The Old Hall Street frontage between Union Street and Chapel Street has retained the jumbled Victorian style, but to our right the façade of the Cotton Exchange was demolished as recently as 1967. The giant stone figure of the

River Mersey has been preserved, a little weathered and perhaps a little surprised at being on the ground after 70 years of standing on the roof.

At the time of writing there is a lot of building activity on Old Hall Street, with a large new hotel on the corner with Leeds Street, and the glorious Albany being resurrected after decades of neglect as apartments. The Albany is one of the best Victorian office blocks in the city, and was designed by J.K. Colling. It was built between 1856 and 1858, and combined offices with warehousing for the cotton trade. The building is very ornate, with richly carved capitals and even keystones, and has a large central courtyard with a famous iron walkway and spiral staircase. It is a popular building in Liverpool.

The narrow street opposite, Fazakerley Street, has been sensitively maintained and has many little businesses on it, although it has the capacity for many more. Spellow Place, at the Rumford Street end, is especially attractive, with a few trees and a cobbled street surface.

The busy junction of Old Hall Street and Chapel Street/Tithebarn Street was once a full crossroads, and the imposing wrought steel gates ahead take us to the smallest of the original seven streets. This is **High Street**, which ran from Castle Street to Old Hall Street. The older Exchange buildings erected in 1803 cut High Street off from the crossroads, losing the sense of Castle Street running through to Old Hall Street. Nonetheless, there is much of interest in this empty piazza. The large round monument was the first public sculpture in the town, and was built in 1813. It dramatically shows Lord Nelson both reaching for high honours and being touched by death, and was designed by Matthew Cotes Wyatt and built by Richard Westmacott. It ventilates the car park beneath, which was originally a bonded warehouse. The Newsroom Memorial opposite, between the gates to Tithebarn Street, commemorates the members of the Liverpool Exchange Newsroom who died in World War One. It was designed in 1924 by Joseph Phillips, and is flanked by two sculptures by Siegfried Charoux. Exchange Flags has been repaved with smart cobbles but, as with Derby Square, it is a shame that this space is not full of cafés and tables.

The High Street/Chapel Street crossroads was the site of the White Cross. The Cross is first referred to by name in 1559, and was a stone cross with a base of five stone steps. It was later one of the first sites in the town to be lit at night; from 1653 a candle-lantern was placed here at night between November and February. Tolls of fruit were usually collected at the White Cross and it had a market as long ago as the reign of Queen Elizabeth I, when vegetables were sold here, especially Formby potatoes, which were highly prized and sometimes given as presents. The White Cross remained intact until 1746, when it was pulled down and not rebuilt. In 1897 the base was discovered during excavations for telephone cables.

Chapel Street is the sixth of the seven original streets. It connects Tithebarn Street with the river, and is named after the small chapel of St Mary del Quay that stood at the bottom of the street. There is a tradition of markets on Chapel Street; the town's first fish market was here, vegetables were traded at the White Cross, cattle were sold here in the 1570s and pigs were bought and sold on Rumford Place.

Chapel Street in 1797. *(LCC)*

Chapel Street was built up with warehouses and merchants' houses, and many survived into the late 18th century to be drawn by Herdman in 1797. Chapel Street itself was once a desirable domestic and business address and James Picton described it as 'a curious medley of medieval remains and modern mansion houses with warehouses interspersed.' Many of these buildings were demolished when the street was widened and straightened in the 1820s.

Modern Chapel Street has the famous Pig and Whistle pub, dating from the late 1700s. In the 19th century it catered for the thousands of emigrants who passed through Liverpool, and the worn brass plate inscribed 'Emigrants Supplied' can be seen inside.

Towards the river stands another of James Picton's handsome *palazzo* office blocks, the Hargreaves Building, completed in 1859 and now the Racquets Club. His greatest office block, Richmond House, stood opposite, but was demolished to make way for another Richmond House which has itself been demolished. A more modern mixed-use building is planned, comprising offices, restaurants, and perhaps apartments.

Most famously Chapel Street has St Nicholas's Church, the parish church of Liverpool, which is well described in most books about the city. The church is open for private meditation, and there is a small café next door. The old churchyard, now an attractive landscaped garden, is usually busy on sunny lunchtimes with office workers sharing sandwiches and staring at the Pier Head below them. There are interesting monuments hidden in the gardens, but maybe none so thought-provoking as the Blitz Memorial overlooking the Strand, with its small boy playing with his aeroplane as his mother holds him on a spiral staircase from below.

Across the churchyard is **Tower Gardens**, named after the ancient Tower of Liverpool, which once stood on the corner of Water Street. This narrow street is too full of parked cars, but it has some interest; the view of the churchyard behind us through the

India Buildings and Oriel Chambers on Water Street.

gateposts, the surging nautical mosaics in the staircase entrance of Reliance House, salvaged from the bombed ruins of an earlier building, and Ma Boyle's Oyster House. This glimpse of an older city, a sooty pinstriped Liverpool, is still busy with local office workers today.

Tower Gardens leads us to **Water Street**. This is the last of the original seven streets on our walk, and today is a busy canyon connecting Dale Street with the Strand. It seems grander than any other of the seven, perhaps because of the incline up from the old waterfront at the bottom. The buildings here are big powerful 20th-century structures belonging to banks or insurance companies. The most imposing of these giants is India Buildings, which occupies an entire city block. India Buildings is a spectacular building, with walls of marble, soaring vaulted ceilings, and huge bronze lamps. It has a great arcade cut through the middle, lined with tiny elegant shops selling chocolates, newspapers, haircuts. Tucked away in one corner, it has one of the most secretive Post Offices in the city. India Buildings was designed in 1923 by Herbert Rowse, described by Quentin Hughes as 'the most influential Liverpool architect of the inter-war years'.

The grand façade of India Buildings is reflected in the many windows of Oriel Chambers across the road. This, the only other building in Liverpool by Peter Ellis, was built in 1864 and still looks futuristic today. Quentin Hughes has argued that it is 'one of the most important buildings in the world' because of Ellis's far-sighted architecture. Oriel Chambers is also very beautiful, with acres of swimming glass and an elegance that many buildings of the time lack.

Four years after designing India Buildings, Herbert Rowse was at work across the road, on the gigantic Martin's Bank building. This astonishing building is one of the sights of the city, and the bank inside probably has more awestruck visitors than customers. At ground level the building is imposing and beautiful but from a distance – say the Anglican Cathedral – the top three or four floors resemble a Roman villa, with clean white walls and a green tiled roof. Yet here too, as with the Town Hall next door, there is an unsettling reminder of the slave trade, with small African children holding bags of gold carved in bas relief next to the main doors.

Opposite Martin's Bank is the old National Provincial Bank, with its fierce bronze lion doors once rubbed by Malay seamen for luck and now surprisingly empty. The narrow street between here and India Buildings is **Fenwick Street**, which leads us back to **Derby Square**. On the corner of Brunswick Street, with its good view of Charles Cockerell's bank building, is the old Heywood's Bank, now occupied by a firm of solicitors but built in 1800 for Arthur Heywood's banking firm. A plaque at pavement height records its history. There are two pubs on Fenwick Street; the famous Slaughterhouse, once supposedly a butcher's shambles and now a cheerful Irish pub, and the Cornmarket hiding its deep leather armchairs and rich Jacobean panelling behind the modern Corn Exchange building, on what was once a ropewalk to the Strand. This 1950s Corn Exchange replaced the Victorian building which was lost in the Blitz, causing the corn merchants to trade in the open air as their predecessors did 150 years before. The end of Fenwick Street has tiny Castle Hill, and a good view of the Queen Victoria Monument at the end of our walk.

Cars on the bombsite on Brunswick Street, 1947. *(LCC)*

The Ropewalks

'[Liverpool] has areas of gloomy ugliness…but it has some fine open squares, too, and some curious backwaters…'
Rupert Croft-Cooke, essay on Liverpool.

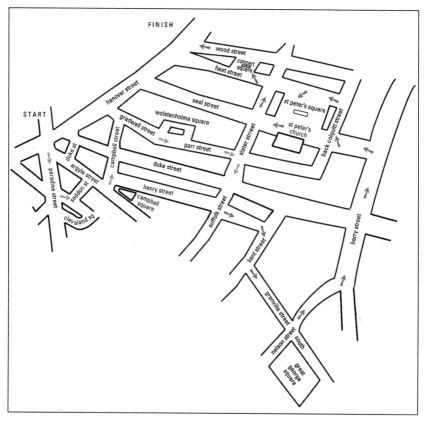

The Ropewalks is a recent name for a corridor of the city centre around Duke Street, roughly between the Anglican Cathedral/Chinatown and the Albert Dock. The district was developed from the early 18th century to provide warehousing and accommodation for the new dock businesses. There were narrow streets of tall warehouses, graceful Georgian squares and churches, and cobbled streets leading to the wharves and quays of the docks, but by the 1980s the area had become run-down, and decades of neglect had turned many of its fine buildings into pigeon-haunted ruins. It was felt that this was an area seen by visitors that needed considerable attention to improve it. Over the last decade a lot of money and time have been spent improving the area and attracting new businesses to the restored Georgian houses of Duke Street, or to lay out new squares and developments, like Campbell Square and Manhattan Place. But at the time of writing this is still an area in transition. The massive new developments are not yet finished, and there are still a large number of derelict Georgian buildings, some with important historical associations.

This is a walk through an urban landscape that has been transformed over the last 10 years. Here the layers of city history seem more present, as if many ages exist simultaneously; Georgian warehouses are used as film sets after decades of neglect, and are then stripped bare and turned into luxury apartments. Students rub shoulders with old drinkers and the new rich. It is an 18th-century industrial landscape built and abandoned, demolished and rebuilt, and only fragments survive in some cases, the bases of sandstone walls, narrow classical arches, the names of slave traders or lost churches.

The area could take a day to explore properly, but the walk itself will take about two hours. It is suitable for children who are interested in history, and there are a number of pubs and cafés which are mentioned in the text.

The walk begins at the corner of Hanover Street and Paradise Street. **Chavasse Park** in front of us is named after Noel Chavasse, son of the city's Bishop and a double Victoria Cross winner during World War One. Today this is a pleasant green space, if a little featureless, but it was once a maze of streets surrounding South Castle Street, one of the oldest of the town streets. As first Pool Lane and later Water Lane it ran down the hill from the Castle to the Sea Lake, the Liver Pool. This was filled in during the late 17th and early 18th century, and the world's first enclosed commercial dock was built on the reclaimed land. The Old Dock proved so successful that it triggered the massive expansion of the docks. In only a century the Old Dock was redundant, and once more the land was reclaimed to build the town's most impressive Customs House. Today the site of the Customs House and the Old Dock is a car park, as the ugly 1960s development that replaced the Customs House has itself been demolished, and the area awaits fresh regeneration as part of the Paradise Street Development Scheme.

The opening of the Old Dock in 1715 led to the expansion of Liverpool across what had been the Pool, and the creation of Duke Street and the surrounding lanes as demand for warehousing and accommodation grew. The reclaimed land around the Dock became built up with warehouses, wharves and sailors' taverns, and became known as Sailortown.

Contemporary artists saw the Old Dock as a Dutch landscape, a second Amsterdam, with narrow warehouses lining the wharves and quays, the Dock and the narrow passage to the river jammed with masts and rigging. Nothing survives above ground level, but in 2001 archaeologists uncovered sections of the Old Dock wall, and it has been surmised that under the present car park the wall is virtually intact. We are standing on what was once the Sea Lake, the lowest geographical point on the walk. Nature does not give up easily, and when the archaeologists were excavating the remains of the Old Dock their boots filled with salt water as the tide came in.

The Customs House was built from 1828 to designs by John Foster, the Corporation Surveyor. It was the largest building in the town, a great sombre Greek temple with large porticoes on each façade. It was relatively undecorated, a majestic, dignified building. The façade onto South Castle Street may have consciously reflected the Town Hall at the other end of Castle Street, as from Derby Square it would have been possible to see both classical buildings, one at each end of the busy street.

The Customs House, 1890. *(LCC)*

Nineteenth-century artists saw the Customs House through the eyes of Canaletto and painted it as a misty presence, lending solemnity and importance to the commercial work of the docks. This Liverpool landmark was heavily damaged during the bombing of 1941 and unnecessarily demolished after the war, a great loss to the city. Only Custom House Lane now serves to remind us of its existence.

Today the roaring traffic of Strand Street and Wapping has amputated the town from the nearest dock, but during the early 19th century this land around the Old Dock was a warren of narrow streets lined with taverns, brothels and grog shops, and the names of pubs marked on old maps of the area carry a whiff of the Victorian sailor's life; the Hanover Spirit Vaults, the Ship Inn, the Black Dog Tavern. The better places provided food as well as beer, as it was forbidden to cook food on board ship in the docks.

Very little survives from this time but the sailors are remembered in Mariners' Parade and behind, in the neglected hollow of the Sailors' Home. This was once a proud replica of a Jacobean country house, opened in 1850 and standing on an island site between the

Liverpool's Sailors Home on Canning Street, photographed from Hanover Street. (LCC)

Custom House and Canning Place, but since the late 1970s it has been home to no more than an unattractive rusty scaffold holding large advertising hoardings. Without this monstrosity, the hollow would have the dignity of an overgrown Roman ruin, its surviving carving and brick cellar vaults visible through the wild flowers. In recent months the ground beneath the scaffolding has been planted with cabbages and other vegetables, perhaps in a mute protest at this ugly misuse of a prime site.

Paradise Street was extended across Canning Place at the end of the 19th century, and leads between two handsome brick buildings to **Cleveland Square**. Before we turn into the square, the car park to our right (on the junction with Park Lane) is the site of the church of St Thomas, demolished in 1905. The low sandstone wall is all that survives of the church grounds.

St Thomas's boundary walls.

The Cleveland Square footscape.

It was perhaps the most beautiful church in the city, an elegant Classical building with a very tall spire, but it is chiefly remembered today as the burial place of Joseph Williamson, the Mole of Edge Hill, although his grave is not marked. The unusual silhouette to our left along Park Lane is the church for the Swedish seamen, designed by the great Arts and Crafts architect W.D. Caroe in 1882.

Cleveland Square is older than it looks, and was named after John Cleveland who was Mayor of the town in 1703 and its MP between 1710 and 1713. Nothing survives of the 18th-century origin of this square, and the remaining Victorian shops are being demolished as they are unsafe. Nevertheless, the square was redeveloped about 15 years ago and now has attractive modern council houses in it, part of a development that stretches behind the Ropewalks up to Chinatown, a reminder that urban living is not a new idea. The council have improved the street surface, the 'footscape', and it is a pleasant mixture of cobbles and reclaimed stone paving slabs.

The narrow **Seddon Street** (behind the surprisingly attractive electricity sub-station) leads us through to **Argyle Street**, and a right turn brings us to **Campbell Square**. This was once Pot House Lane, and is the site of one of the town's old potteries, a thriving industry for Liverpool in the late 18th and early 19th century. A walk around here today is very different from a walk even a decade ago.

This is the heart of the regeneration of the Ropewalks district, and the gently decaying warehouses have been transformed into smart bars and luxury apartments. The

Campbell Square, 2004.

old tarmac has gone, replaced by modern setts and kerbstones, attractive and yet suitable for traffic. The area won a Royal Town Planning Institute Award for Conservation and Urban Regeneration in 2002. There is modern street sculpture here by Stephen Broadbent, a cross between a cowbell and a Trojan helmet, and most impressively the old Bridewell has been saved from dereliction and is now a pub-restaurant. It sells good food and beers, although there are very few windows on the inside.

Yet a lot of the older warehouses were too ruinous to be restored, and so for safety's sake they have had to be demolished. Something of the atmosphere of the area was demolished with them; the survivors have been cleaned and saved, but too many of them have security cameras on them and security fences guarding private gardens and car parks. Henry Street winds up the hill to our right, but we walk past the Bridewell and along **Campbell Street** to **Duke Street**.

Duke Street and Duke Terrace, photographed by the author in 2004.

Duke Street is the spine of Ropewalks, a wide street connecting Chinatown with Hanover Street and Paradise Street to our left. The town's merchants built houses and warehouses here from the mid-18th century to live and trade in the area nearest the docks, their fine houses facing Duke Street with their counting houses or warehouses behind in Henry Street or Parr Street. It is named after the Duke of Cumberland, whose troops defeated the Highlanders of Bonnie Prince Charlie on Culloden field in 1746. The street was laid out in the early 18th century and still has some Georgian terraces on it – there is an almost complete block between Campbell Street and the old warehouses at the bottom of the street, to our left. Duke Street has many historical and cultural associations. John Keats is supposed to have stayed here while seeing his brother George off to America in 1818. The American painter John James Audubon was entertained in 1826 at 87 Duke Street by William Roscoe and William Rathbone, whose family lived on the street for many years. John Bellingham lived on Duke Street, and is famous for being the only man to assassinate a British Prime

Campbell Street, restored to former glory.

Minister; he shot Spencer Perceval in the lobby of the House of Commons in 1812. The poet Felicia Hemans was born at 118 Duke Street, and the celebrated painter Sarah Biffin died at 8 Duke Street at the age of 84. When he was American Consul to Liverpool in the 1860s, Nathaniel Hawthorne lodged at No.186 Duke Street, and wrote of his son sliding down the banisters. Too many of the buildings are still derelict.

'The view up Duke Street,' wrote William Moss in 1796, 'has always a pleasing effect, even to an inhabitant who sees it daily.' In the late 18th and early 19th century it was a smart and fashionable district, but many of the rich who built elegant houses here in the 18th century were slave owners or traders, and little Campbell Street ahead and behind us is named after George Campbell, mayor of the town in 1763, whose fortune was built on sugar and slaves.

The continuation of Campbell Street takes us to **Gradwell Street**, and a right turn leads us past gigantic warehouses and small businesses into **Wolstenholme Square**. This Georgian square was once far more fashionable an address than Duke Street, and although it seems to have faded very quickly and become built up with warehouses and businesses, there are still some weather-beaten Georgian survivors.

Wolstenhome Square.

A new cut-through to Duke Street is called Tunnage Square after the barrel businesses that supplied local breweries. This is an area that comes alive at night, when the streets are full of clubbers and drinkers. The huge Cream nightclub empire started life in the Nation nightclub in Wolstenholme Square, and this has been a square of clubs for many years. The square had an avenue of trees behind it called the Ladies' Walk, one of a number of 18th-century promenades in the city, and had a garden of trees in the middle. Recent street improvements have restored the illusion of this garden.

Parr Street, at the top end of the square, takes us to **Slater Street**. This is a street of bars and pubs, alive at night with drinkers spilling out onto the pavement. On the corner of Parr Street opposite is one of the oldest buildings in the district, until recently home to a small restaurant called Tito's. It is dwarfed by the ugly car park and office block behind it, where the Liverpool branch of the Arts Council is situated. The fine sandstone building on the right has been recently renovated for the shipping company Bibby's, but it was built by John Foster senior in 1800 as the Union News Room, and for a time in the 1850s was the town's first public library. The pub opposite, the Monro, is an 18th-century survivor, and was once a merchant's house.

Turning left behind the Monro onto **Henry Street** leads us past the Chinese cultural centre, known as the Pagoda, and a street of the old businesses that used to inhabit the area before the regeneration; small printing works, car workshops, cabinetmakers. On **Kent Street** at the top stands Manhattan Place, a huge new development of apartments that typifies the new face of the city. A massive Victorian wall has been incorporated into the ground floor, neatly illustrating the layers of history in this area. Turning left onto Grenville Street, the open grassland ahead was once the churchyard of St Michael's Church. This huge sandstone church was built in the early 19th century, and resembled St-Martin's-in-the-Fields in Trafalgar Square. St Michael's was destroyed by German bombing in 1941 and pulled down in 1946. A new church of St Michael in the City occupies some of the land, but it is a shame that the churchyard is neglected and vandalised. On the corner of Cornwallis Street opposite is a grand new building for the City College, revitalising this rather solemn Victorian street. Next door are the old workshops for the blind, in an ornate Gothic maze of a building recently used as artists' studios and workshops but currently awaiting redevelopment.

Grenville Street takes us to **Great George Square**, laid out in 1802 and now a sad shadow of its former self. The square was built as houses for merchants and professional men, and was later used as lodgings by shipping companies, providing accommodation for people in transit to North America. Most of the Georgian character has been lost, but there are a few embattled survivors and the large central park is currently being redeveloped. To our right is **Nelson Street**, named after the hero of Trafalgar; his captain, Hardy, is commemorated behind Nelson Street, in the post-war developments.

This is the heart of Liverpool's Chinatown, which once stretched to Cleveland Square at the foot of the hill, but is now confined to the streets around Berry Street and Nelson Street. Liverpool has the oldest Chinese community in Europe. The city has belatedly made some effort to celebrate this by defining the area with rather kitsch Chinese-style street furniture; lampposts have golden dragons twirled around them and little lanterns as lamps, the rubbish bins have subtle pagoda roofs, even the bollards and pay-and-display boxes are brightly painted in red, gold and green.

Perhaps more seriously, the street signs are now written in English and Chinese characters, and huge bronze lions guard the streets on stone plinths. The unique

Chinese dragon in the heart of Liverpool's Chinatown.

Nelson Street and the new Chinese arch.

character of Chinatown has recently been celebrated by the erection of the gigantic arch at the top end of Nelson Street, an instant landmark and symbol of the regeneration of the area.

But the full regeneration of the area has a long way to go. Much of the Ropewalks district is still rundown or derelict, and **Berry Street**, the first busy city centre street seen by visitors from the south of the city, needs a lot of work to make it as smart as it could be. There are new bars and restaurants here, as well as the older Chinese businesses, but the street is often dirty, and there are still boarded-up premises. Yet some dereliction is deliberate. At the far end stands St Luke's church, bombed in 1941 and deliberately left roofless as a memorial to the nearly 4,000 Liverpudlians who died in the Blitz. 'The bombed-out church' is a Liverpool milestone, often used for reference or directions. The grounds now contain a large monolith, commemorating the dead of the Irish Famine, with text in English and Irish Gaelic. The gardens are well-maintained and a good place for a picnic lunch.

Seel Street runs in a straight line from Berry Street to Hanover Street at the bottom of the hill, and is named after Thomas Seel, who owned land between here and Hanover Street in the 18th century. The street is younger than Duke Street and was laid out through fields and market gardens in 1790. Seel Street is presently being redeveloped, and there are still empty Georgian buildings at the very top of the street, their fanlights thickly encrusted with two centuries of paint, their firmly-bolted doors used as billboards by the city's flyposters.

The Blue Angel nightclub on the left, once a Beatles haunt, was the birthplace of Dr Henry Duncan, Liverpool's first medical officer, who did so much to improve the city's health. A plaque above the door commemorates him. The Irish pub opposite, Pogue Mahone's, with its rich

No.79 Seel Street.

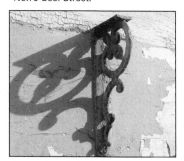
Ironwork and shadows.

The Royal Institution on Colquitt Street, built in 1799.

gargoyles over the door, was for many years called Doctor Duncan's in celebration of his birthplace.

One of the town's earliest synagogues stood a little further down Seel Street on the junction with Colquitt Street, and again a plaque commemorates this. The synagogue was designed by Thomas Harrison, architect of the Lyceum Post office on Bold Street. Few of his Liverpool buildings survive and this site is now occupied by the rear of a telecommunications building, although recent street improvements have dignified the site with a small line of oak trees.

To our left on Colquitt Street stands the dignified red-brick Royal Institution. This was built as a house and warehousing by Thomas Parr in 1799, and is one of the very few surviving Georgian homes with warehousing attached. Parr Street, to the left of the house, runs down the hill towards Wolstenholme Square. The house was occupied for many years by a distant ancestor of the University, the Royal Institution, which was established in 1817 to promote the arts, literature, and the sciences. The Royal Institution was the venue for the first exhibition of John James Audubon's wildlife paintings in Europe, and Charles Dickens and the poet Thomas Campbell gave readings here in the 19th century. Fittingly enough the building later became part of the University, and is now occupied by a charity. Colquitt Street Technical College, in front of the Royal Institution, is part of the City College, and many of the bars and pubs around here cater for students. The La'go on the corner of Seel Street and the Masque venue behind serve good food during the day.

Back Colquitt Street, off Seel Street to our right, now has a tree-lined alleyway running to join Ropewalks Square on Bold Street, part of a new network of routes across the landscape created by the Ropewalks regeneration. The new building on **Fleet Street**

Redevelopments on Seel Street.

ahead of us is the huge FACT development. This arts complex has a number of cinemas and a gallery, as well as a smart café/restaurant called Rear Window, and is one of the great success stories of modern Liverpool's regeneration. FACT – the Foundation for Arts and Cultural Technology – is housed in the old Mantunna tea building, which is why the bar and apartment complex next door is called the Tea Factory. (On Wood Street behind is one of the best pubs in the city, the Swan, a tiny noisy bikers' bar serving giant sandwiches and good beer, the only place in the city we are likely to see a biker reading Marcel Proust, seemingly oblivious to the crashing rock music around him.)

A little further down Fleet Street is one of the area's new squares, built in the late 1990s on the site of an old iron foundry. **St Peter's Square** is a well-designed urban space with big bronze boxes as seats, and birch trees. It is named after the old Catholic church opposite, on **Seel Street**, which, when it was built in 1788, stood in open fields.

The Georgian properties between the square and Slater Street have, at the time of writing, not been redeveloped and stand empty and largely derelict. The pub on the corner, the Marlborough, named after the victor of Blenheim, has had a facelift recently. This is one of the city's stranger pubs, architecturally; a great box of a place with tall iron columns. The pub has opened a sandwich hatch onto Seel Street, and now serves fresh food right onto the street.

Slater Street is at the very heart of the Ropewalks nightlife. It is a street of bars and pubs, and attracts hundreds of mainly young people to drink at night. On summer weekends it resembles the worst sights of Ibiza, with hundreds of drunken young people filling the street. Yet arguably the regeneration of this district began here, with the opening of the Baa Bar and the development of Concert Square in the early 1990s. The remainder of Seel Street, between here and Hanover Street, is marked for redevelopment and work has already begun on transforming empty or derelict warehouses into luxury apartments.

Many long-established small businesses, which give the area its charm, are also threatened by this regeneration, and no amount of expensive flats or brash pubs can compensate for the loss of an old bookshop or a shop providing musicians with drum kits and rehearsal space. Feelings run high here; it is felt that property developers are given *carte blanche* to improve an area as they see fit without thought given to what

Old and new near Concert Square.

makes an area attractive in the first place. **Concert Square**, between Fleet Street and Wood Street, has interesting footscapes, with cobbles and old railway sleepers used to good effect, and many of the old warehouses have been given new life. And yet the sole reason to go there is to drink; no thought has been given to the quality of the regeneration here, and Concert Square has a poor reputation in the larger city. But then this area has always been a drinkers' quarter; on Victorian maps a number of pubs are marked in what would become Concert Square; the Manchester House, the Globe Inn, the Prince of Wales Inn. And in the mid-19th century we would have walked past the Seel Street Brewery to reach here from Seel Street. It is perhaps an area built on drink and short-term pleasure, although the drink-sodden sailors and prostitutes have given way to students and office workers.

Wood Street is the oldest of these streets running to Hanover Street, and was a country lane at the end of the 18th century. It became the poor relation of Bold Street, and was built up with the back entrances and store-rooms of the smart shops. Today it has been regenerated, with some success, and is now a continuation of the drinking haunts and nightclubs of Concert Square. It had some of Liverpool's first modern city-centre apartments, and it also has the Open Eye Gallery, the city's premier photographic art gallery, as well as a decent Italian restaurant. The foot of Wood Street has a basement Irish pub and some modern bars and leads us back to **Hanover Street** and the city centre.

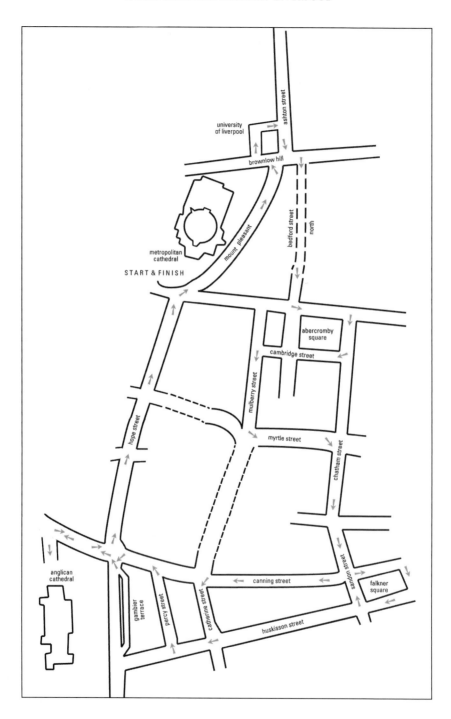

WALK 3
Liverpool Bohemia

'Strange tides of life here in the city rise/with light and shadow…'
Edmund Burke, *'Liverpool'*.

This walk explores the streets between the two cathedrals, which were laid out from the early 19th century onwards as Liverpool expanded. The town's merchants moved away from the idea of having a warehouse attached to their homes and needed bigger premises. Their social aspirations grew too, and they left the dockside areas of Duke Street for grander developments on the hill overlooking the town. The very rich moved to Everton, but many moved to the 'new town', the squares and elegant streets of what is now Liverpool 8. The wealthy stayed for roughly a century, and even before World War Two many had left these big draughty houses for properties with gardens in Childwall or Woolton, or moved to the fresh air of the Wirral. The big terraced houses were broken

Architectural details on the Irish Centre, which has been empty for over a decade.

Liverpool's Roman Catholic Cathedral.

up into flats and bedsits or became lodging houses, and the roads out from Catherine Street fell into seediness, with a reputation as the red-light district of the city. But its nearness to the Art School and the University meant that the area was popular with students and artists, and these crumbling, sooty Georgian streets became the home of painters, musicians, poets and writers. And it is surely one of the ironies of Liverpool's history that in the mid-20th century many of the houses built by merchants grown wealthy on slavery became home to the city's black community.

The walk proper starts at the **Metropolitan Cathedral**, the Catholic cathedral of the city famous for its two cathedrals, but it is worth having a quick look at the building next door across Great Orford Street. Everyone in Liverpool knows this small classical building as the Irish Centre, but it was built in 1816 as the Wellington Rooms, although admittedly the Iron Duke was Irish. It was intended as an Assembly Rooms for the town, a place for meetings and dances and social occasions, a very Georgian idea, suggestive of an anxious rustle of crinoline and the grin of a Mr Darcy. It was designed by Edward Aikin, who also added the grand stone portico to the façade of the Royal Institution, and the entrance porch here was originally open. This was found to be draughty and so it was bricked up. The building was the Irish Centre for over 30 years, but has now been empty for nearly a decade. It is possible that the porch will be opened once again, however, as it has been announced that the building's new owners hope to renovate the building and reopen in time for St Patrick's Day 2005.

The Metropolitan Cathedral is a strong landmark building, designed by Frederick Gibberd and opened in 1967. The cathedral is emphasised now by a brand new

The rooftops of Mount Pleasant.

Surviving fragments of Lutyens's Cathedral.

ceremonial staircase from Hope Street, which gives dignity and lift to the central drum, with its huge glass lantern designed by John Piper. From being gently mocked as Paddy's Wigwam and the Mersey Funnel, the Metropolitan Cathedral is now accepted and even respected as a beautiful and very spiritual building, quiet and peaceful; on sunny days the stained glass panels in the walls send sheets of colour across the plain limestone walls.

Below the modern cathedral is the titanic ghost of a far bigger building. Edwin Lutyens designed a Byzantine structure that would have rivalled the Anglican Cathedral and been the biggest Catholic cathedral in the world, apart from St Peter's in Rome. The giant piazza that the modern building sits on (like a landed spacecraft, say unkind critics) is the ground plan of a building that was never built because of World War Two and escalating costs, but Lutyens did build huge vaults and a small number of underground chapels. Nothing survives of the huge Victorian workhouse which stood here before being cleared for the cathedral, although the archdiocese offices on Brownlow Hill used some of the buildings until very recently.

Lutyens's immense piazza, right at the top of the hill, gives good views in all directions. To our right, over the Irish Centre, the slim spire of the Oratory of St Philip Neri, now part of the Liverpool John Moores University complex, rises above the rooftops. To the left, Mount Pleasant sweeps around in front of us, and at the junction with Hope Street stood the tavern and bowling green where William Roscoe was born in 1753, when this was almost open countryside. The piazza is also the best place to see the splendid Victoria Buildings, designed by Alfred Waterhouse. This is the original red-brick university; high Gothic walls and tall windows, and a great landmark tower more suited to a Prague church than a British university.

On **Mount Pleasant** (or around the corner on **Brownlow Hill**) we can see some of Sir Edwin Lutyens's surviving work for the cathedral; hacked into the bedrock or exploding from it, the stonework is still deep and crisp, and gives some idea of the immensity of scale of the building. From Brownlow Hill we can walk through an arch cut through the Victoria Building, and Waterhouse's love of detail is evident even at eye level as we walk into the university precinct. This dark square is usually full of parked cars and students walking to lectures, but it has a small green heart with benches and

Victoria Buildings, 2004.

The red-brick Gothic architecture of the university.

flowerbeds. According to Quentin Hughes, the Arts Faculty building in front of us was probably designed by F.W. Simon, the architect of the lost façade of the Cotton Exchange on Old Hall Street. It is a strong building and defiantly Classical next to its industrial Gothic neighbour, but a building dated 1913 for modern eyes has a sadness about it; a sense of things coming to an end and of youth being wasted, an unfortunate echo in a landscape designed for education.

The University has many attractive buildings, and an afternoon could be spent wandering the streets and parks of the campus to see them. On **Ashton Street**, for example, underneath the Arts building through the handsome arch to our right, is a huge complex built by Alfred Waterhouse as the Royal Infirmary in the late 1880s. Here there are yet more of his handsome red brick walls and terracotta details, sweeps of neat slate roofs, and heavy

The arch cut through to Ashton Street.

tiled interiors. The University has only occupied the Infirmary for a short time and much of the complex is still in need of renovation, but much has been done after nearly 20 years of dereliction.

From Ashton Street we cross Brownlow Hill again. The church to our left on the hill is St Mary's at Edge Hill, and the rising ground marks the edge of the Great Heath that once separated Liverpool from the surrounding villages. Ahead of us is Mountford Hall, part of the Students' Union, designed initially by Charles Reilly in 1910, although the building has been extended and adapted over the years. Reilly was the University's first Professor of Architecture, and an advocate of Greek Revival design. His handsome building now forms the core of the biggest Students' Union building in Britain. To our left, hidden away in an undistinguished concrete piazza, is the Augustus John, the first of the University's pubs. The painter spent time in Liverpool as the guest of the University, teaching and painting the University's dignitaries, but in his writings he confessed that he was happier sneaking off into Chinatown to try and take opium. 'Liverpool, commonly considered a dull, ugly and commercial city,' he wrote, 'for me abounded in interest and surprise.' His painting of Charles Reilly hangs in the University Art Gallery in Abercromby Square.

Alongside Mountford Hall is **Bedford Street North**, an area developed, not always successfully, by the University after World War Two. The old Georgian streets disappeared or were gradually blurred into pedestrianised walkways and landscaped car parks, and the early 19th-century houses were replaced by modern faculty buildings

Mountford Hall and Victoria Buildings.

Abercromby Square, laid out in the 1820s.

surrounded by shrubs and young trees. This route should therefore be greener and softer than it is, but the hard lines of Bedford Street North have survived, and lead us through to **Abercromby Square**. (The blurring of Chatham Street North has been more successful; this street has almost disappeared into the campus, and its line is marked now only by an avenue of trees.)

Abercromby Square is the heart of the University, and the prettiest of Liverpool's many squares. During the summer the lawns at its centre are dotted with students reading or talking in the sunshine. The square was laid out in the 1820s, and behind the elegance lay the fear of insurrection. Quentin Hughes argues persuasively that the houses were built by rich men who had seen the effects of riots in Liverpool from the 1770s onwards, and 'the ditches of the houses…had vertical scarp walls and counterscarp walls modelled on contemporary military architecture.' The square has a suitably military name; it is named after Sir Ralph Abercromby, who defeated the French at the battle of Alexandria in 1801. The mobs of sailors and clerks have long gone, and the square now houses many University libraries, studies and meeting rooms. It also has the University Art Gallery, the quietest in the city; it has an excellent collection of paintings and ceramics, clocks and Russian icons donated or willed to the University over the years. Two of John James Audubon's paintings are here, as is Augustus John's portrait of Charles Reilly.

On a plinth on the other side of the square is Barbara Hepworth's strong modern sculpture *Square with Two Circles*. It dominates the lost stretch of Chatham Street that

Barbara Hepworth's sculpture, *Square with Two Circles.*

once passed through Abercromby Square in front of St Catherine's Church, which was designed by John Foster. The University demolished all this side of the square in the 1960s, and while the modern Senate House reflects the classical lines of the rest of the square, it is regrettable that the entirety of the square was lost. Ahead of us is a luckier University church, the Welsh Methodist chapel built in 1861 and now called the Chatham Building. The corner of Abercromby Square has what must be the oldest pillar box in the city, and the fierce sculpture on the slope in front of the modern Sydney Jones Library is *Red Between* by Philip King.

The small **Cambridge Street** connects Abercromby Square with **Mulberry Street**, and another of the University pubs, the Cambridge. Opposite, on the site of the modern student accommodation, was the first parish cemetery in the city, laid out in the early 19th century and quickly out-dated. There were also almshouses on Cambridge Street, built in 1787 by the corporation before the grid-pattern streets were laid out, and they can be seen on old maps, strongly at odds with the surrounding roads.

On the sweeping corner with Myrtle Street and Catherine Street stood the Children's Hospital, famous for its open wards and welcoming garden frontage. The site is now occupied by the City College Arts Centre. The Liverpool Gymnasium stood next door at the beginning of the 20th century, and its clearance for a car park revealed a cholera pit, perhaps an extension of the graveyard used for the dead of a cholera epidemic of the

The Chatham Building, formerly a Welsh Chapel, built in 1861.

Cambridge Street Almshouses, 1910. *(LCC)*

1840s. This site is now the Varsity bar. Like many of the city's large buildings the Liverpool Women's Hospital across the road on Catherine Street has been turned into homes, this time for students.

Myrtle Street to our left leads us to Myrtle Parade, and Bedford Street South on our right. This is the street that we explored in the University, blocked off now by modern University buildings. This length of the road through to Upper Parliament Street shows how the street used to be; a wide road of elegant 19th-century properties. Set back from the road and with attractive iron balconies, the two houses at the end of Bedford Street have been recently restored. They were derelict for many years, but in 1971 were used in the film *Gumshoe*, with Albert Finney and Billie Whitelaw.

At the far end of Myrtle Parade is **Chatham Street**, named after William Pitt the Elder, the first Earl of Chatham, who died in 1778. These are some of the oldest buildings in modern Toxteth. George Melly's family lived here for many years, and Charles Reilly, the architect and Professor of Architecture, lived here for three years in the 1920s. His house is marked with a plaque.

The extension of Chatham Street is **Sandon Street**, where modern townhouses have been built in a style sympathetic to the surrounding Georgian architecture. Sandon Street leads us to **Falkner Square**.

Falkner Square is the quietest of Liverpool's squares, and the only one to survive intact. It was laid out in 1835 by Edward Falkner, a property speculator, and was built in almost open country. His terrace on Upper Parliament Street was considered so far away from the town that it was nicknamed Falkner's Folly. Falkner Square is a peaceful green

View of Falkner Square, 2004.

Views of Falkner Square, 2004.

space surrounded by stuccoed houses on streets lined with mature trees; occupants of the top-floor flats look out over a sea of green. Architects have been drawn to these quiet Georgian streets; as well as Charles Reilly living on Chatham Street, Peter Ellis lived in Falkner Square. The park in the centre has recently been refurbished, paths restored and benches smartened up. It has a small monument to the black merchant seamen who died during World War Two; a long way from the other nautical monuments at the Pier Head, but maybe more at home here, near the city's black community.

This is where Georgian Liverpool ends. Until the 1960s the streets of houses with their columns and porches used to run up to Smithdown Lane and Aigburth Street, and the amputated remnants of Upper Canning Street and Upper Huskisson Street can be seen on the Grove Street side of the square. These were cleared 40 years ago for the strikingly unsuccessful Falkner housing estate, which, derelict and burned, lay half demolished for many years in the 1980s and 1990s. Now the site is occupied by the Liverpool Women's Hospital, and the blue roofs of this bright modern building can be seen at the end of the stumped streets.

The wide residential streets that lead out of Falkner Square are called Canning and Huskisson Streets, named after politicians of the early 19th century. They are lined with tall houses, now being restored after decades as flats and bedsits. They are as smart as any similar development in the country, and it is a good sign that this architecture is valued once more. Both cross quiet Bedford Street again, on its way to Upper Parliament Street to our left. We take **Canning Street**, and have a famous and much-photographed view of the tower of the Anglican Cathedral rising over the roofs. At the

Canning Street and the Anglican Cathedral.

The grounds of St Philip Neri church, Catherine Street.

junction with Bedford Street we cross the road past the trees of the German church. This was originally established to provide Lutheran services for German sailors, and moved to a Victorian church here in the 1930s, replacing it with the modern building in 1959. St Bride Street and Little St Bride Street alongside the church are often used by filmmakers wanting cobbled streets and gaslights, and have been used in many films and television dramas.

The busy road ahead of us is **Catherine Street**, one of the main routes in to the city from the southern suburbs. The church opposite on the right is the only Byzantine church in the city, opened in 1920 as the church of St Philip Neri, and now the Catholic chaplaincy for the University.

Next door is one of the most famous hidden gardens in the city. Through the railings can be seen the Garden of Our Lady, built on a bombsite after World War Two by the priest from St Philip's. Behind the church is the tiny, sturdy Blackburne Terrace, built in 1826 and still one of the prettiest terraces in the city.

Further along Catherine Street is another imposing church, St Bride's, which opened in 1830. It is a fine classical building with imposing columns and a large,

Blackburne Terrace.

unkempt, green space around it. Behind is **Percy Street**, a beautiful street of sandstone houses that Quentin Hughes calls 'little Edinburgh' because of the style of its architecture.

John Lennon and Stuart Sutcliffe shared a flat at No.9 Percy Street, and also lived for a time in Gambier Terrace. Their bohemian squalor was documented by the *Sunday People*, long before the Beatles became famous.

From Percy Street we turn left onto **Canning Street**. On our left is **Gambier Terrace** which was built to exploit the views over the river and the Wirral to the hills of Wales.

Details of some of the buildings to be seen in Canning Street and Percy Street.

The Anglican Cathedral at night, photographed in 1959. (LCC)

But from 1904 the Anglican Cathedral was built on the small St James's Mount in front of it, and residents now have the finest views of this great building in the city. The Cathedral and the cemetery can be reached by walking down Duke Street straight ahead. The cemetery is older than the Cathedral. It was laid out in a disused quarry, and modelled on Père La Chaise in Paris, with great ramps and catacombs and mournful trees. The graves were cleared in the 1960s to make an urban park, and the graveyard is now a peaceful Arcadian landscape, with tombs dotted across the grass, and birds singing in the trees. There are many prominent Victorian citizens here, sea captains and politicians, merchants and priests, but perhaps none so important as Kitty Wilkinson, whose selflessness (in taking in the washing of cholera victims, for example) was largely responsible for the creation of the first public wash-houses in the city. She is a largely unsung heroine of Liverpool, but the Cathedral has a portrait of her in stained glass. The little domed temple in the middle of the graveyard once held a statue of William Huskisson, killed by Stephenson's *Rocket* on the opening day of the Liverpool & Manchester Railway, which has been removed for safekeeping. Most poignant perhaps are the giant gravestones recording the deaths of the orphans from the Bluecoat Hospitals.

The **Anglican Cathedral** is one of the tourist sites of Liverpool, and amply documented in many books about the city. It is an astonishing building; great towering walls of red Woolton sandstone, a tower more like a Hindu temple than a Gothic cathedral, and clusters of columns on the transepts that for all their colossal size ripple like hung curtains. It also has a pleasant tearoom burrowed into the building, with an outside terrace overlooking the cemetery below.

Walking back up **Duke Street**, we pass the Liverpool Institute for Boys, once one of the great schools of the city. Arthur Askey attended the Institute, as did Peter Sissons, the newsreader and journalist, who remembered playful fights with George Harrison. Neil Aspinall, the Beatles' road manager, studied at the Institute with Paul McCartney, and it was McCartney's drive and impetus that reopened the building in the 1990s as the Liverpool Institute for the Performing Arts (LIPA).

Hope Street is the final leg of the walk. This is one of the most attractive streets in Liverpool, with many of the original Georgian façades intact and handsome buildings replacing the lost ones. There are many bars and restaurants and some of the city's giant cultural institutions. The modern building on the right is now part of LIPA but was built as part of the Art College, the old entrance of which can be seen on the corner of Mount Street. Its most famous old boy has to be the disruptive and anarchic John Lennon, who was more interested in music and girls than art, but the Art College had a good reputation at the time for both students and tutors.

There is a fine view down Mount Street through the city to the river, and the thought of travel and distance is emphasised by the suitcase sculpture by Amanda Ralph on the pavement. The neat terrace on the right was the home for many years of the Liverpool poet Adrian Henri, and his old house looked out onto the giant porch of the entrance to the Mechanics' Institute, the forerunner of the Liverpool Institute.

The suitcase sculpture by Amanda Ralph on the pavement in Mount Street.

The French chateau over the wall to our right is another old Liverpool Institute, this time for girls. The oldest part of the building can be seen on Blackburne Place. This was the country retreat built in 1785 by John Blackburne, who was mayor in the 1760s. It was later the girls' school and attended by Edwina Currie, among many others. It is now called Blackburne House again, and is a technology centre for women. It has been beautifully and imaginatively adapted to its new use, and has a friendly café in the basement.

Blackburne House, now a technology centre for women.

Down tiny Rice Street to our left is the Cracke, a pub visited on the pubs walk, but well worth another visit for a glass or two of beer. It has one of the best beer gardens in the city, and was once the local for John Lennon and Stuart Sutcliffe and their friends and tutors from the Art College.

The old London Carriage Works on the corner of Hope Place is one of the new 'designer hotels' in the city, reflecting the new money and tourism that Liverpool is attracting. Behind it is the Unity Theatre, Liverpool's only venue for fringe theatre and serious local writers and performers, an excellent venue to see the best national small-scale theatre companies on tour.

Another view of Blackburne House.

Stone garland on the Art School, photographed by the author in 2004.

On the busy junction with Hardman Street and Myrtle Street stand the two Philharmonics. Opposite is the fantastic confection of the Hotel, while on our right is the disapproving Art Deco solemnity of the Philharmonic Hall, home to the city's Philharmonic Orchestra. The pub, which is explored on the pubs walk, also has occasional musical performances, while perhaps in revenge the Hall has started selling beer and food. Hardman Street, going downhill on the left, has many bars and fast food places catering for the students and young people who drink here. Behind is Maryland Street, with the Students' Union of the city's newer university – we are in student land again. The Georgian terrace on our right has the famous Casablanca Club, last of the city's black clubs and now owned by a consortium of ex-dockers. The Catholic cathedral and its new staircase can be seen clearly for the last stretch of the walk, past another quiet row of Georgian houses, now offices and workshops. On the right at the end is the Everyman, once a church, a chapel, a cinema, and now a theatre. It also has a bistro downstairs and serves good beer and food. It is popular with students, artists, and the actors and audiences from the theatre upstairs and is a good place to end the walk.

WALK 4

The Three Parks Walk

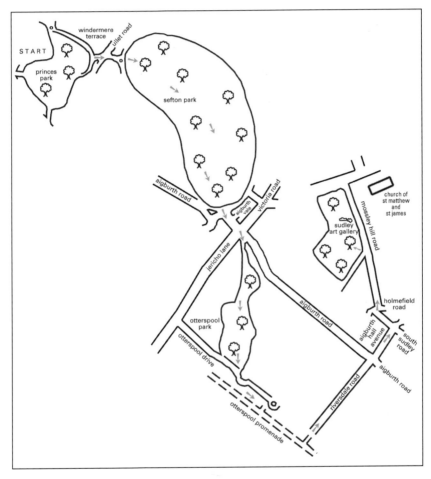

Liverpool is fortunate in the amount of green open space it has. The city centre is ringed with large open spaces forming a green necklace: Princes Park, Sefton Park, Calderstones Park, Newsham Park, Stanley Park (not to mention smaller green spaces and cemeteries), all within easy reach of the city centre. This walk covers three parks in the south of the city and ends on the top of Mossley Hill in Allerton, and was originally devised for the BBC Radio 4 programme *Ramblings*. It was broadcast in April 2001 when the programme was looking for urban walks to avoid the countryside, much of which was closed due to the foot and mouth outbreak. The start of the walk, **Princes Park**, can be reached by the 80 or the 86 bus to Princes Avenue or by the 82 to Aigburth Road.

Princes Park was laid out in 1842 by Joseph Paxton, the architect of the Crystal Palace, and is one of the oldest parks in the country. Belvidere Road and Devonshire Road around the park have some very attractive Italianate houses, mostly divided into apartments, and have been a quiet part of Liverpool's bed-sit land for 40 years. But after some years of decay this is slowly becoming a desirable place to live once again, with even Princes Avenue being renovated.

The park attracts many species of birds to its lake and mature trees, which also shelter bats and rabbits, which can be seen in the early mornings and evenings. It has winding paths and thick shrubs, and is popular with fishermen, local dog walkers and children from the local schools. It was not originally a public park, however, and the gates were locked at night, with access being restricted to the owners of the surrounding villas. These helped to pay for the development of the land, and private access was seen as a perk. A hidden gate into an empty park is not always seen as an asset these days, but the grand villas themselves are very attractive, with the newly restored buildings on Sunnyside being especially smart.

The path around the park leads us to **Windermere Terrace**. This is a very quiet part of the city, with crumbly roads and peeling paint as the Victorian buildings grow old gracefully. Many of these Italianate villas are now apartments. The Catholic girls' school Bellerive and its associated convent also occupy two or three of these handsome houses, and the terrace reverberates with the squeals of released children at about four o'clock. The road on our right takes us to **Ullet Road** again. This is an extremely old road, possibly as old as the city itself, one of the old farm lanes of Toxteth, and runs under the trees to Smithdown Road.

The busy road to our left is Sefton Park Road, the extension of Lodge Lane. The Lodge guarded the 13th-century royal park of Toxteth, and its remains form part of the Victorian house visible through the trees on our left. Over Ullet Road we pass one of the park lodges erected in the 1870s when Sefton Park was laid out, and crossing the busy Aigburth Drive, we enter the park through the unusual Gothic screen of sandstone and granite columns, like left-over pieces of a Victorian church, which in spring is attractively underplanted with bedding plants. Ahead of us the tall obelisk commemorating Samuel Smith MP marks the entrance to the park proper.

Sefton Park is the greatest park in Liverpool. At 233 acres it is the biggest and also the grandest, laid out in 1872 after a national competition. It has great roads lined with houses around the outside, and many features of a Victorian park; winding paths and plantations of trees, a bandstand, an aviary, a large lake, even a pirate ship and a replica of the Peter Pan statue. The park is one of the best places for an outing or a picnic in Liverpool, and its huge fields make it popular with footballers, walkers, kite flyers and day-dreamers happy to watch the clouds sail by. There are herons here, turtles in the small lakes, many types of ducks and great skeins of Canada geese in the winter. There are even supposed to be goldfish, perhaps released by children anxious to set them free, and there is certainly a huge golden field of daffodils planted by the Marie Curie cancer charity as a symbol of hope.

The long straight path has had its Victorian lamp posts restored, and they lead to the café and the statue of Eros. This is the centre of the children's part of the park, with the aviary to the left of the café and the Peter Pan statue beyond the aviary. The path straight ahead to the right takes us to the Palm House. This great Victorian glasshouse has been restored and is once again open to the public, with a visitor centre and giant hothouse plants.

An afternoon could be spent walking from one end of the park around to another and exploring the sights, but the path to the right of the huge bronze fountain takes us onto the series of little lakes and waterfalls that runs through the park like a watery spine, criss-crossed by stepping-stone paths. Past the ornate bandstand the land drops away, and the large lake appears, which was created by damming a large stream that rises in Wavertree. The lake is popular with fishermen, who used to tell a story of a giant pike, big enough to take small ducks, that lurked in the old streambed at the bottom of the lake. The path follows the lake around to the Aigburth Vale entrance to the park. In the summer there used to be boats for hire at the little jetties, and there is still usually an ice-cream man here today. The old drinking fountain, with its thick columns and dolphins,

Daffodils in bloom in Sefton Park, 2004.

Sefton Park water fountain.

is a pretty feature of this end of the lake, and the huge Gothic screen guarding the roadways into the park has been recently restored. It is planted with bedding plants each year.

We are now in **Aigburth Vale**, one of a number of 'vales' in the city. The highway ahead of us is Aigburth Road, which connects the airport and the south end of the city with the centre. Aigburth Vale is a busy shopping area, with a long line of shops facing Aigburth Road. At the lowest point of the road ahead of us there is a small and somewhat dingy underpass, heavily decorated with rococo swirls of graffiti, but we are soon through it and up the steps on the other side. Ahead of us over Jericho Lane (another reminder of the Puritan settlers) are the thick woods of **Otterspool Park**.

Otterspool Park is one of many parks in Liverpool that are the remains of the landscaped parks and woodlands surrounding country mansions. Here, as in Childwall Woods or Camp Hill, the sweeping paths and many of the landscaped features remain while the big house has disappeared. There are unusual plants too among the native giants, acers and rhododendrons and great firs, and strange delicate trees with feathery red autumnal leaves. The estate was formed from the valley of the large stream, romantically called the River Jordan by the Puritan settlers, which can be seen – or heard – gushing in a culvert over the wall before we reach the gates. As a small river valley, the park is low-lying and with the thick woods it can be damp. The main path ahead of us leads straight through the woods and is well paved, but if the weather has been dry for a few days, take the narrow unpaved path to the right and follow it across the top of the steep side of the valley until it rejoins the path by the railway bridge. This is a quieter route over thick, fallen leaves, and we are more likely to see woodland birds such as woodpeckers or treecreepers in these trees. This is one of a number of paths laid out at Otterspool in the 1860s and the 1920s; there are also giant mysterious sandstone ramparts and buried paths under the rhododendrons.

The beech trees to the left of the main path, where Aigburth Road is seemingly held back by a great stone wall, are truly gigantic. Protected from strong winds they have been allowed to grow to astonishing heights, and are among the tallest trees in the city.

Otterspool was laid out as an estate by the Moss family at the end of the 18th century. George Stephenson is supposed to have been a guest here during the building of the Liverpool & Manchester Railway in the early 1830s, and to have built a model of the line on the old bed of the Jordan. The only railway here now is the old Cheshire Lines track to Garston and Hunts Cross, which leaps across the park on a great sandstone bridge. Here the upper path from the entrance rejoins the main route and, before it turns and descends the slope, Otterspool Station can be seen through the trees. This is now a private residence, but it is the site of the other lodge for the old hunting park of Toxteth,

New birch trees in Otterspool Park.

Riverbed in Otterspool Park.

and it is said that many of the sandstone blocks lining the paths in Otterspool are the remains of this building. The great astronomer Jeremiah Horrocks was born in this lodge in 1619 when it had become a farmhouse.

The old observatory in Otterspool Park.

After the railway bridge the park has a great open field to the left and the path curves gently to the right. A cobbled lane off to the right leads to what used to be stables and farm buildings for Otterspool House, which stood on the site of the café. This is now closed and boarded up, which is a great pity, but Otterspool is not one of the popular parks of Liverpool, and is quiet even on summer days. Perhaps the quiet woods and old rhododendrons seem closed in and claustrophobic, and wide open spaces too far apart, but for walkers interested in birds, or plants, or buried landscapes, Otterspool is a treasure.

Ahead of us now is the **Otterspool Promenade**, but the sunny dell in front of the café, with its rose bushes and picnic benches, is a popular spot for picnics. The manicured trees at the top of the incline seem to stand against the skyline as if nothing is behind them, but be warned – there is a road on the other side that can be busy.

In contrast to the park, Otterspool Promenade is always busy with families on summer afternoons. The Prom has big sunny fields, popular with picnickers, footballers, kite flyers and walkers, and is far enough from busy roads to be safe for children.

To our right there is a new pub, the Otter's Pool, which welcomes children and serves

The path down to the Promenade.

An empty Otterspool Promenade, which has views to the Welsh hills, Birkenhead and Ellesmere Port.

good food all day. Crossing the road at the small car park we can see the carved slate plaque which records the creation of the Prom in 1950, built on top of the city's refuse.

From here we walk down to the river.

The Mersey here is at its widest, as muddy as the Amazon and as dynamic; when the tide is in we could almost touch the water, but when it is out the muddy riverbed is 30 feet below us. On clear days there are great views to the blue Welsh hills, and up and down the river to Birkenhead and Ellesmere Port.

Follow the Promenade until a large car park and a small house appear on the left. This is really a sewage station for the huge new Aigburth sewer, cleverly disguised as a doll's house. The road behind the car park, **Riversdale Road**, has the unusual distinction of having two cricket grounds on it. The road leads past Riversdale College, currently under threat of closure as part of local education reordering, to Aigburth Road and the second cricket ground, the more famous Liverpool Cricket Club. We are back on Aigburth Road, and crossing it we come to **Aigburth Hall Avenue**. This is a quiet suburban area of semi-detached houses laid out in the 1920s and 1930s, but many of the boundary walls here are older and are made of sandstone.

On our left is Stanlawe Grange, a barn possibly built in the 1200s for the monks of Stanlawe Abbey, who farmed land here. It has been a private house since the 1960s. Before the 1920s this was an area of small mansions set in parkland, and Aigburth Hall Road to our right has two gently crumbling Italianate villas, survivors of this Victorian landscape.

There is another survivor of the demolition of this Victorian landscape at the end of **South Sudley Road** on our left. This is a quiet road of interwar semi-detached houses, but it takes us to the heavy sandstone gates belonging to a house called Holmefield. The estate is now a part of the I.M. Marsh PE College, but turning right and then first left up the narrow road alongside the estate, some of the old house can be glimpsed through the trees. We are now on **Mossley Hill Road**, marked on maps from the 1760s. It used to cross a stream at the bottom of the hill before becoming Outacre Lane and heading towards Garston. At the top of the hill, another set of gates for Holmefield can be seen on the left, where Barkhill Road runs up the hill. This is another old lane, named after a farm which once stood between here and Aigburth Road.

At the top of the hill the landscape opens out. To our right are the Holt Fields, and ahead of us the road runs unsteadily on towards Mossley Hill church. This is the spine of Mossley Hill, and to our right the view extends across the valley of Brodie Avenue to the rising ground of Allerton and Woolton. The strong tower of All Hallows' church rises from the trees, and further to the right we can see the Italianate tower of All Souls' church on far away Mather Avenue. After 70 years, the trees in the gardens below us are mature, and the red roofs of the houses seem to pepper thick woodland. It feels very rural up here; tall trees, sandstone walls, open fields and the towers of distant churches.

The small gate in the wall to our left takes us into **Sudley,** and the path around the boundary wall, which winds pleasantly through the trees. This is one of my favourite places in the city, a good place for a walk, or a think, or an hour with a book on a hot day. Sudley was once the estate belonging to the ship-owning Holt family, and it was left to the city by Emma Holt in 1945. She was George Melly's aunt, and the jazz singer has many memories of visiting her when he was a boy. Emma Holt also left the city her family's collection of paintings and sculpture, and today Sudley is one of the quietest art galleries in the city. It has a fine collection of 18th and 19th century paintings, and there are works here by Reynolds, Gainsborough, Turner and Rodin. The estate has not been modernised, and there are still many of the outbuildings and gardens associated with a small country house. Holt Fields and Sudley are given over to playing fields, but Sudley in particular is big enough to be able to avoid the footballers and walk through the belt of thick woodland around its edges. In spring there are carpets of daffodils, and crocuses among the tall trees surrounding the house, and in the autumn there are many different types of mushrooms in the damp soil, and redwings migrated from Siberia feeding on the fields. There is a tearoom open at weekends and on Bank Holidays, and Sudley is a peaceful location for a thoughtful walk or a picnic.

This is the top of Mossley Hill, and the end of the walk. There is a lot to see in this wooded Victorian suburb. The huge Gothic church of St Matthew and St James on our right, for example, or the surviving mansions on the other stretch of Mossley Hill Road in front of the church, some being restored, some still divided into bedsits. To our right Rose Lane dips down towards Allerton Road and has a good pub, the Rose of Mossley, on it, as well as cafés and sandwich shops. Trains back to the city can be caught at Allerton railway station at the bottom of the hill, or a bus stop for the 80 bus can be found just past the pub. To the left is Aigburth Vale, where any number of city-centre bound buses or the 'Smartbus' (Nos 1 or 5) can be caught.

WALK 5

Back Streets and Shopping

'Liverpool is the Pool of Life.'
Carl Jung

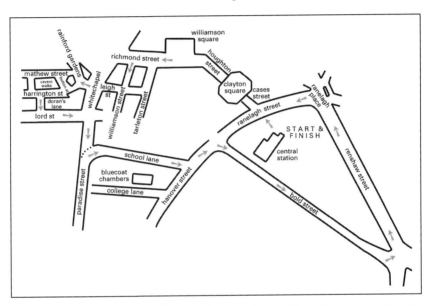

Liverpool has a secret pattern of quiet back streets that enables walkers to cross the city without fighting the traffic. Here the rush to pedestrianise the city in the 1960s and 1970s has been a rare success; some are lifeless corridors connecting one bigger street with another, but some are lively and varied lanes with a vibrant mixture of small shops, corner pubs, and unexpected architecture. They are not as celebrated as they should be, these alternative pathways through the city, and far more could be done to enhance and improve them, but their success and appeal is proved by their use; these streets are free of traffic, but are always busy with people. Many Liverpudlians choose to cross their city by these narrow streets, and to outsiders and local urban walkers alike they are a vital and interesting way of exploring the city.

This is a walk for shoppers and people interested in the hidden side of city life, although it is probably impossible to satisfy both curiosities at once. Liverpool has too few public toilets, but the walk is well equipped with cafés, coffee shops, pubs and restaurants.

The walk begins in **Central Station**. This 1980s shopping mall caters mainly for people rushing to and from the railway station, as Central is the main city centre station for the local railway network. Crossing Ranelagh Street we enter short **Cases Street**, where something of the street life which once filled the city centre has been preserved. There are four or five business including three pubs between Ranelagh Street and the doors of Clayton Square, and the street usually has at least one street stall in it, selling fresh fruit and vegetables. Cases Street is both somewhere to go and somewhere to use to get somewhere else, almost a definition of a healthy street.

Cases Street, leading to Clayton Square.

Clayton Square was once a real city square, built between 1745 and 1785 by the Clayton family, and many of the local streets – Cases, Elliot, Parker – commemorate families linked to them through marriage. The quiet residential square began to go downhill in 1822 when Elliot Street was cut through from Lime Street, and the houses were turned into hotels and offices. Modern Clayton Square is a huge glass shopping mall, built when the old square was regrettably torn down in the 1980s. It has the usual high street stores that can be found in most British cities, and some more unusual shops upstairs. Business stalls have been set up in the corridors of the Square, recreating the kind of street life that is going on outside. Clayton Square is soulless and single-mindedly commercial, but it also has a piano bar, a good place for a coffee, and its great glass dome has added an interesting feature to the city's roofline.

The continuation of Cases Street leads us to the ghost of Clayton Square; the space between Clayton Square and Houghton Street resembles a city square proper, although it lacks focus and dignity. Parker Street and Elliot Street were once very busy with traffic,

Clayton Square, 1922. *(LCC)*

but have been pedestrianised for many years. To the right is the unloved hulk of St John's Precinct, rebuilt over 20 years ago after a disastrous fire. Here too a real street environment has been recreated indoors with glitzy lines of rather ordinary shops and eating places, but it does have the virtue of having a real market; in the large central hall is the descendant of the market founded by King John with the borough in the early 13th century.

The exterior of St John's Market, photographed in 1909. *(LCC)*

To our left, Houghton Lane and Tyrer Street run through to strange Leigh Street, now used almost exclusively for deliveries to the huge John Lewis store. It will take generations before Liverpudlians refer to it as anything other than George Henry Lee's. Liverpool's top department store is a very attractive building, with many unusual entrances and exits, rich wooden doors, fine mosaic floors and rich wedding-cake plasterwork.

Houghton Street is dominated by St John's Beacon, a giant flue for the heating fumes from the precinct. The Beacon is one of the symbols of the city, and with the two cathedrals is a strong feature of the Liverpool skyline. In the 1970s the Beacon had a restaurant in it, which gently revolved in order to give diners a view of the city hundreds of feet below them. Today it is offices and studios for one of the city's radio stations, which seems peculiarly fitting, although its inherent ugliness has not been lessened by the erection of a huge metal frame around it, supposedly for digital broadcasting.

Next to Lee's on Williamson Square is the Liverpool Playhouse, once the country's oldest repertory theatre and now amalgamated with the Everyman Theatre on Hope

Street. The Playhouse performs more traditional plays than the Everyman, and has a fine reputation.

Williamson Square and nearby Williamson Street were laid out in the 1740s by the Williamson family. On the northern side stood the Theatre Royal, opened in 1772 and designed by John Foster. It was the largest theatre outside London when it was built. In later life it was the Union Cold Storage, and it had a famous round façade jutting onto Williamson Square. When architect Ken Martin came to extend the Playhouse in the late 1960s he deliberately echoed this drum shape in his work; the Theatre Royal has gone, but the glass extension to the Playhouse holds its memory. The square is currently undergoing yet another transformation. The building of the Liverpool FC store and neighbouring shops in the 1990s restored the traditional look of the square, which for many years looked out at the bus shelters across Roe and Hood Streets, with its fourth wall missing. But Williamson Square is a wasted opportunity. Apart from the Liverpool FC shop, the shops seem second-rate; you can buy burgers, second-hand clothes, cheap shirts. One of the city centre's best squares, it should be linked properly with the rather dead space outside Clayton Square and have the feel of an Italian piazza, with a weekly street market, flower stalls, and cafés making the most of the sunshine, the passers by, the life on the streets. The new development will have a modern fountain, which is a step in the right direction.

Richmond Street opposite has much of the life that Williamson Square lacks. It is one of the most attractive streets in the city, a lively, jostling place, with sandwich bars and hot pie shops doing a roaring lunchtime trade. It is named after the Richmond family,

Williamson Square, 1946. *(LCC)*

St John's Beacon and Richmond Street, one of the most attractive streets in the city.

who had long links with the town – Sylvester Richmond was mayor in 1672. You can buy paper clips here, climbing boots, a suit, a newspaper, 20 cigarettes. The shops and businesses are jammed into a hotchpotch of city buildings, austere 1920s classical or elderly sooty Gothic with a hint of Venice. The Richmond pub is a good place to spend an hour over a glass or two and just watch the people passing by, as is the Queens, a handsome building on the corner of Williamson Square, once frequented by the actors from the Playhouse.

For many years **Williamson Street** was the opposite of Richmond Street; it was a dead canyon, with blank concrete walls and the sides of larger shops all it had. In recent years this ugly trend seems to have been reversed and more shops are opening, yet this is still a poorly developed area. Tarleton Street, which runs from Church Street to Williamson Square, is dull and inhospitable, but there are one or two old buildings here, the old Yates's Wine Lodge, coffee shops, even a pavement café, but the eastern side of the street is the grim wall of Marks & Spencer's. Strangest and most lost of all is Leigh Street, which has been allowed to die; it runs from Whitechapel to Parker Street near Clayton Square, but over recent years it has been steamrollered. The stretch between Whitechapel and Williamson Street is dirty and vandalised; between Williamson and Tarleton it is empty and featureless. Here Leigh Street disappears into Marks & Spencer's, like a river running underground, only to reappear on Basnett Street between the two blocks of John Lewis's; here again it has been built over, and the street splutters to a halt on Parker Street. Tarleton, Williamson, Leigh – these streets are not rough or dangerous; there is no life here at all, but with some thought and creativity the whole area – which is already pedestrianised – could be an interesting and lively place, connecting Williamson Square with Church Street.

Turning right down Leigh Street from Williamson Street we come to **Whitechapel**.

This was once the Pool, the semi-tidal creek that ran from William Brown Street to the river at Canning Place. It has been forbidden to cars for some time, and is one of the major walking routes for this end of the city. To our right it runs past Queen Square, a modern piazza of hotels, restaurants and bars, to the roundabout of the Queensway Tunnel at the foot of St John's Lane and William Brown Street; to the right it becomes Paradise Street at the junction with Church and Lord Streets. (There used to be a Liverpool joke: 'leaving the Church on your left and the Lord on your right, you enter Paradise...') Whitechapel is a part of the major shopping routes through the city, and so we cross it to enter **Button Street.**

Cavern Quarter warehouses.

This has been designated the Cavern Quarter, the district surrounding the old Cavern Club, and is a good example of streets that work. The streets are narrow and the old warehouse buildings are tall, but Button Street and Rainford Gardens are lively and interesting. The warehouses were built for the fruit trade; **Rainford Gardens** was once a market garden running down to the Pool, built by Peter Rainford who was mayor of the town in 1740. Some attention has been paid to the street surface, the footscape, although this good work is ruined by the utility companies, who dig the streets up but do not always replace the paving. The footscape is not perfect but the area has sculpted chairs, ironwork signs, unusual paving. This is an exceptional area as it attracts tourists, but there is no reason why all of the city centre's back streets and secret routes should not be as good as this. The recent development Cavern Walks is a mixed blessing. It is an ugly building with its elegant shops squashed by 10 or 12 floors of offices, and the ground floor feels cramped and claustrophobic; but it has rejuvenated the area, and there are now art galleries, cocktail bars and designer clothes shops in the wide floors and cellars of the old fruit warehouses.

Mathew Street has a long association with Liverpool's popular culture. In the 1950s and 1960s the Cavern Club was a venue allowing first jazz and then rock 'n' roll bands an opportunity to perform, most famously the Beatles. Ten years later the empty warehouses were taken over by proto-punk thinkers who had massive plans for the cultural renaissance of the area, and the famous Eric's club opened, as important to the bands of the 1970s as the Cavern had been a decade earlier. From Eric's and the scene that grew up around it came many of the great Liverpool bands of the 1970s, linked by

Cavern Walks, with its smart shops.

Modern Mathew Street.

shifting band members and a belief in the noble street ideals of punk rock. Mathew Street has chosen not to remember them, and instead the street is a shrine to the Beatles, whose original Cavern Club was demolished in 1972. There is a fine statue to John Lennon's surly Hamburg days, and an older and finer one by Arthur Dooley on the wall above. The large building on North John Street with the sooty stone walls and heavy granite columns is due to become a Beatles-themed hotel, which could be very good or very bad. Perhaps it is churlish to snipe; the area has been regenerated through Cavern Walks and the Beatles bring in many tourists and fans each year. The Mathew Street Festival in August sees the streets jammed with thousands of fans, and hundreds of bands playing almost continuously for three days. And yet there is a lot more to the city's musical heritage than Beatles' songs.

Through **Cavern Walks** with its smart shops and truly amazing atrium we come to **Harrington Street**. This has not been well developed and is a blank and unsophisticated corridor from North John Street to Button Street. It is an old street, and was once known as Castle Hey, indicating perhaps that it was the orchard or croft surrounding the Castle; above North John Street it curves to join Castle Street, as if still following the line of the moat. James Picton mentions the interesting fact that the art of printing onto pottery from engraved plates was first discovered by John Sadler, an engraver and china manufacturer, on Harrington Street, and that at one time Josiah Wedgwood sent some of his delicate chinaware here to be printed.

Modern Lord Street, pedestrianised but underused.

Doran's Lane is a narrow alleyway that once ran between the gardens of the houses on Lord Street, and has been here since the late 1600s. Today it is a blind cut-through to Lord Street.

Lord Street is one of Liverpool's major shopping streets, and has been for 200 years. It was built in 1688 by Lord Molyneux, who then owned the Castle, and named after him. It suffered badly in the Blitz, and most of the buildings are designed in a bland 1950s Modernist style, although there are some pretty Gothic survivors, such as the Pudding Bowl Café, to our right. Lord Street has a major department store, but the street seemed to lose its heart and style after World War Two, so that most of the shops – jewellers, travel agents, stationers – seem too small for this grand street, and would be better suited in small back streets. There are smart clothes shops here, but the shop units are too small and the street seems fussy as a result. In recent years the city authorities have used its wide pedestrianised site for a series of European markets, where unexpected Dutch flower bulbs can be bought, rare French garlic, sizzling German sausages. As a market venue this street works very well, and it is an excellent use of an otherwise rather dull route.

We are now at the crossroads of Church Street, Whitechapel, Lord Street and **Paradise Street**. All are forbidden to cars, and all are busy with walkers and shoppers most of the time. Only in the early evening, as the city refreshes itself before going out for the night, are these streets quiet, which is a good time to examine the many attractive buildings in more detail.

Paradise Street seems to end abruptly, because at present it has the huge bus station on it. The area between here and Canning Place has been designated the Paradise Street Development Area and over the next few years will be massively redeveloped. The empty streets and car parks behind College Lane will be swept away, and given new life. Many new shops will be opened, including one or two 'flagship' stores, and hopefully the whole area will be rejuvenated.

Opposite the bus station is narrow **College Lane**, which leads up to Hanover Street. This lane is named after the town's first grammar school, which stood near here. The school was attached to St Nicholas's Church and was established before the Reformation of the mid-1500s, and the College Lane building became a forerunner of the Bluecoat School.

At the time of writing many of the old streets on our right have no buildings on them and are used as car parks. Hopefully this will change when the area is redeveloped, and yet something of the character of these narrow streets will be retained. There are very old warehouses on College Lane, one of which still has its merchant's home facing Hanover Street. This was common practice in the 18th century, when merchants lived alongside their businesses.

The Bluecoat Arts Centre is scheduled to close for massive refurbishment, and it is possible that this whole area will be inaccessible during the redevelopment. If this is the case, we can use School Lane to see the front of the Bluecoat and reach Hanover Street.

The Bluecoat Arts Centre.

School Lane has a few shops on it, but is given life by the Quiggins complex of records-and-clothes shops in the old County Palatine building. This is unmistakeable, as it always seems to have shuffling groups of young people dressed in floppy black outside. They are Goths and skateboarders, and during the week they are at college doing A-levels and thinking about university. They are invariably polite. Quiggins also has a large friendly café, but the whole complex might disappear in one regeneration.

There are a small number of shops at the top of School Lane, but some very old empty shops were regrettably demolished at the

Architectural detail on the Quiggins complex.

Hanover Street end about five years ago, and not replaced. School Lane could be a very interesting urban street; it has a rich variety of tall narrow brick office buildings and warehouses, and hopefully as it is developed its potential will be realised.

Hanover Street is an unremarkable city street named as an act of homage to the royal house of Hanover. It marked the edge of the town in the early 1700s, and up the slope towards Berry Street were fields and gardens. Turning left, we pass through Waterloo Place to Bold Street.

The old bank on Bold Street, now a bar.

Bold Street has been 'Liverpool's Bond Street' for over 100 years. The long straight street with its terminus of St Luke's Church has many fine buildings and many good shops on it, as well

88

Bold Street, 1953, decorated for the celebrations for the Coronation of Queen Elizabeth II. *(LCC)*

Façade of one of the buildings on Bold Street, Liverpool's Bond Street.

Tiled floor in Bold Street.

as bars and clubs. It is largely pedestrianised, although the traditional street pattern of kerbed pavements and cobbles was restored after some years as a 1970s pedestrianised street with concrete flags and raised flowerbeds. This has meant that most people still use the pavements in preference to the street. You can buy Italian kitchen gadgets here, fashionable clothes, puppets from Indonesia, new books and second-hand books; blue glass from Afghanistan, cameras, rare vinyl records, heavy Thai furniture and fresh fruit.

Bold Street leads us to **St Luke's Place**, dominated by the tower of the church. To our

St Luke's Place, 1932. *(LCC)*

right is Berry Street and Chinatown, but to our left is **Renshaw Street**. This is known locally as 'Rapid Hardware Street' as one side is entirely occupied by the famous Liverpool DIY store, the only place in the city centre to buy nails and hinges, drill bits, bathrooms, carpets, wash basins, paint… The other side of Renshaw Street is a pleasing Victorian hotchpotch of buildings, a little scruffy, but the street is always busy as this is a major route into the centre from the south end of the city. There are many fascinating businesses here – collectables shops selling Art Deco china, old army coats, Beatles toys, tweed jackets, Star Wars models; renovated pubs, Indian food stores and restaurants, the unlovely Stanley Casino. The most attractive shop is the Olive Tree, selling Arabic cushions and Moroccan

St Luke's Church.

lamps, tiny jewelled tables and elaborate textiles. The street is dominated by the Central Hall, built in a massive red-brick Art Nouveau style by the Methodists and now a complex of bars, its stubby towers and swirling curves accentuated by well-designed security grilles and modern mosaic work.

We are now at **Ranelagh Place**, named after the pleasure gardens that once occupied the site of the Adelphi Hotel. This glorious building may not have the prestige it once had, but it is the city's most famous hotel and a very handsome building. It seems to grin cheekily at the solid Lewis's building, which frowns back as if disapproving of all that

Central Hall, Renshaw Street, opened 1905.

sunny limestone opulence. Lewis's is another of the city's great department stores, and on the corner is the famous 'exceedingly bare' statue by Jacob Epstein symbolising Liverpool's rebirth after the war. The bronze panels depicting childhood are also by him. Behind Lewis's is **Central Station**, and the starting point of our walk.

WALK 6
The Forum

'The esplanade in front of St George's Hall might be called the Forum of Liverpool, being the receptacle of most of the statuary of which Liverpool can boast…'
Sir James Picton

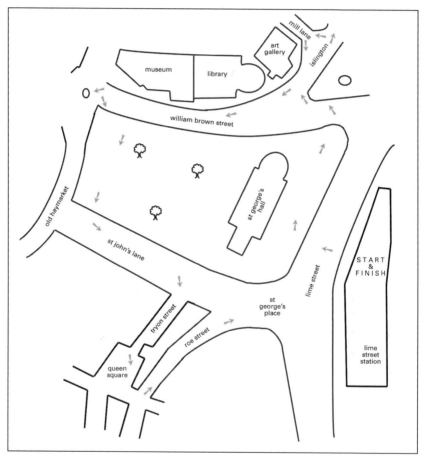

Liverpool has always thought of itself as a classical city. In the 18th century the mediaeval streets were widened and straightened, and the Georgian town built Assembly Rooms, the Town Hall, classical warehouses and terraces of grand houses. Painters saw the Mersey in Venetian terms, with ships sailing past the great domes and columns of the waterfront, and small skiffs resting on the gentle Adriatic swell to watch them. William Roscoe saw parallels with the Florence of the Medicis, and Victorian Liverpool imagined itself as a patrician city inspired by the artistic capitalism of the Florentine Renaissance. Architects such as James Picton, Charles Cockerell and Thomas Harrison designed banks, offices and warehouses with pillared halls and large Italianate windows to let in more light. But Liverpool's love of the classical extended beyond its architecture, and seeing itself as a Renaissance seaport; in the mid-19th century it created a civic forum.

From the building of St George's Hall in the late 1830s, the land on what is now Lime Street and William Brown Street was cleared and re-imagined as a civic space. It happened slowly, gradually, but over the next 70 years the city built art galleries and museums, law courts and monuments to itself and its own sense of solemn Victorian civic pride. Today there is such a wealth of classical buildings here that it can become

abstract, a cut-and-paste vision of gigantic columns, fluted or plain, heavy walls pierced by huge windows, great pediments and arcades of yet more columns. This is the obvious place for the city's cenotaph, remembering the dead of two world wars, and the many smaller modern monuments in St John's Gardens behind.

But here, as elsewhere in the city, the present has overwritten the past. The 'forum' area was once known as the Great Heath, the uncultivated lands outside the town. James Picton says that the Great Heath must have closely resembled Bidston Heath across the river, 'a long slope of barren rocky soil,

View down William Brown Street, 2004.

declining to the west, covered with whin bushes and heather'. Liverpool did not cross the tidal creek known as the Pool in any strength until the early 1700s, and the end of Dale Street was known as the town's end; there was a Townsend Cross here from at least 1575 and the bridge over the Pool was called the Townsend Bridge. In 1564 the bridge was in need of repair, and so must already have been in existence for some time. There was also a stream running down from the Moss Lake, a huge marshy area at the top of the hill, which ran into the tidal creek near Byrom Street and ran under the Townsend Bridge before flowing along Whitechapel and joining the Mersey nearly a mile away.

The Fall Well, site of Lime Street, 1771. *(LCC)*

There were probably windmills here from at least the 16th century, and Picton refers to a storm in 1565 that destroyed many windmills in the town. From the early 1600s Townsend Mill stood on the higher ground up the slope, and during the Civil War, Prince Rupert's engineer-soldiers bombarded Liverpool for 18 days from trenches and earthen gun platforms, which stretched from the Townsend Mill to Copperas Hill. William Brown Street was known as Shaw's Brow, which was an unmetalled road running uphill from the Townsend Bridge. There were almshouses on the south side of Shaw's Brow from 1684, which were extended in 1692. The town began to expand and build on the land over the Pool in the early 18th century; more almshouses were built here from the 1720s, and an early Baptist chapel was built in 1722 on Byrom Street.

The town's first Infirmary opened, with 30 beds, in 1749 on Shaw's Brow. The Sailors' Hospital opened in 1752 as two wings of the Infirmary, which stood on the site of St George's Hall facing the Walker Art Gallery. 'The general effect of the buildings was pleasing and agreeable,' wrote James Picton. 'They were of dark red brick with stone dressings, with a cupola over the centre of the Infirmary, and smaller ones over the wings.' The hospitals were set in large gardens, big enough to hold a lunatic asylum which opened in 1789. At the Roe Street end was the Fall Well, at one time one of the few sources of clean fresh water in the little town, and its name is commemorated in a modern pub built into the St John's Precinct near Queen Square. In 1783 a church dedicated to St John the Baptist opened on the Great Heath, on what is now St John's Gardens; it is from this unloved church that the Precinct, the Lane, and the Gardens take their names.

At the same time, the late 1700s, industry began to spread across the landscape. In addition to the windmills that were erected further up the slope to catch the breeze, ropewalks were established alongside the Infirmary, a marble yard opened on the site of the modern railway station, and potteries were built on Shaw's Brow running down to

Aerial view of St George's Hall and Lime Street, 1930s. (LCC)

Pottery Kiln at Shaw's Brow.

The 300-room North Western Hotel.

the creek. Limekilns were built on the railway station site by 1745 and the new road alongside the incomplete Infirmary was called Limekiln Lane. They belonged to William Harvey, who reluctantly moved his kilns to the North Shore in 1804 when it was felt that the smokes and smells were bad for the Infirmary's patients, and from about 1790 the road became Lime Street. At about the same time stagecoaches began to run from Dale Street, up Shaw's Brow towards Prescot and eventually London.

Nothing of this landscape of hospitals, windmills and light industry survives today. The Townsend Mill was demolished as long ago as 1780, the hospitals were too small by 1826, and the Lunatic Asylum was taken down in 1835. In 1839 the foundation stone of St George's Hall was laid, and the development of this area into the forum was begun.

The walk starts at **Lime Street Station**, the third station on this site. John Foster built the first for the new Liverpool & Manchester Railway terminus in 1836 when the trains descended from Edge Hill by gravity. The station presented a long classical wall to **Lime Street**, pierced by arches for entrances and exits, and was described by James Picton as 'somewhat stately and grandiose'. Some of the yellow brick wall of the second station, built only 15 years later, can still be seen on Lord Nelson Street.

The present huge station building was opened in 1871, and incorporated the 300-room North Western Hotel. The Gothic spires and turrets are typical of the work of Alfred Waterhouse, and this is another of his Prague rooflines, with swirls of close-fitting slates like sleek armour, steeply pitched roofs and tiny spiky turrets. The high walls have

Another view of the North Western Hotel, designed by Alfred Waterhouse.

gigantic industrial Gothic arches, now freshly cleaned of decades of soot to reveal acres of pale golden stone. At night the rooms glow with light as they are halls of residence for Liverpool John Moores University, and inhabited again 40 years since the Hotel closed.

Emerging from the station we are confronted with St George's Hall, one of the great buildings of the city and internationally renowned for its architecture and engineering. The architect, Harvey Lonsdale Elmes, was only 23 when he won the competition to design a concert hall and Assize Courts for the town. Liverpool is justly proud of this huge building, and most books on Liverpool mention St George's Hall in great detail. Yet since the law courts moved out, the Hall has been something of a white elephant for the city. There are occasional events or trade shows, but Liverpool lacks the imagination to do anything special with St George's Hall; to have it at all seems enough, this curiosity to be admired but not used. And yet; it is currently being cleaned, and in the evening sunlight its height and great columns are once again breathtaking.

St George's Plateau has been appropriately planted with lime trees, and the street surface laid with cobbles in a beautiful series of interlocking curls and circles that echo the Minton tiled floor inside the building. The

Detail of the cenotaph.

St George's Plateau footscape.

Detail of the Wellington monument.

lampposts are heavy globes supported on fantastical dolphins, and there are giant sleepy lions in front. The cenotaph was erected in the late 1920s, and has bronze panels of mourners in fashionable clothes; their mourning becomes timeless, eternal. The forum is an appropriate location for the city's cenotaph, but Liverpool has many smaller war memorials in almost all its districts.

Over **William Brown Street** is the single column of the Wellington Monument, with the figure of the Iron Duke far above. The bronze for the monument is supposed to have come from French cannon captured during the Napoleonic wars, and the names of forgotten battles are written in huge letters on the great panels at its base; Toulouse, Nivelle, Quatre Bras. There are bronze distances marked out by the Board of Trade, too, old imperial measurements of perches and inches.

The Steble Fountain is a cast-iron fountain named after Colonel R.F. Steble, who was mayor in 1874. It marks the site of the Townsend Mill, which is remembered by Mill Lane, between the Walker art gallery and the old County Sessions House. Mill Lane now leads to a private car park, but it used to lead to Hunter Street which ran down the hill to Byrom Street. Hunter Street is now one of the main roads to and from the Mersey Tunnels and the roads

The Steble Fountain and the Wellington Monument.

The County Sessions House on Islington.

behind the Sessions House are always busy with traffic. Mill Lane itself has small 'rockeries' of carved stone in the grounds of the art gallery, and perhaps some of these fragments are from bomb damage during World War Two.

Looking down William Brown Street the slope to our right was once dotted with the beehive shapes of pottery kilns, and there were rows of almshouses at the bottom of the hill. Ahead of us was the Sailor's Hospital and the Infirmary in well-laid out gardens, and behind was **Islington**, which ran up the hill towards Everton and West Derby. Modern Islington is a road of extremes; for most of its length it is a featureless sprawl of concrete, three or four lanes of traffic thundering in each direction, with bland landscaping instead of real buildings. But the little stretch which joins it to William Brown Street has the County Sessions House and the Walker Art Gallery, elegant classical buildings on stone pavements and cobbled roads.

The Walker Art Gallery is generally accepted as one of the country's best provincial art collections. Michelangelo and Raphael sit nonchalantly outside, their limestone faces blurred by the Liverpool weather, inviting us in. The collection is not enormous, not daunting, and a peaceful afternoon can be spent gazing at smoky Dutch landscapes and fragments of mediaeval statuary torn apart at the Reformation. There are rooms of tiny icons and great Victorian pieces, works by Millais and Holman Hunt and Rembrandt, as well as more modern work and the winners of the John Moores exhibition, held every four years. The County Sessions House next door is now part of the National Museums

Weathered stonework on the County Sessions House.

and Galleries on Merseyside, and its great wooden courts are open to the public. Its ornate face is crumbling with the weather of a century, but its doorways (like the Bridewell on Cheapside, reminiscent of the forbidding prison architecture sketches of Piranesi) are as forbidding as ever.

The great drum of the Picton Reading Room neatly realigns these classical streets, and joins Islington with **William Brown Street**, the old Shaw's Brow. The Central Library is the main library of the city, with the Reading Room its most obvious feature; the main entrance is hidden away like a second thought, beneath the towering Roman temple of the Liverpool Museum. This was the first of the forum buildings to be laid out on William Brown Street. It was severely damaged by bombing during World War Two, and has a modern museum behind the Victorian façade. The Museum is a part of every Liverpool childhood; the Lion locomotive and the old Overhead Railway carriage in the basement, the aquarium, the huge rockets and totem poles, the elegant rooms of Roman, Egyptian and Greek antiquities. On the top floor next to the planetarium and café was a room of clocks, from Chinese water clocks to delicate timepieces built in Prescot in the 1700s. Some of this has been dispersed to other newer museums in the city, and the Liverpool Museum has taken the opportunity to modernise and expand into the old Technical School at the bottom of the hill. Edward Mountford, the architect of Lancaster Town Hall, designed this staid but quite formidable building at the very beginning of the 20th century. Perhaps cheered by the perky bronze lampposts, which are delicate and

The great drum of the Picton Reading Room.

beautifully decorated, it seems to turn a blind eye to the horrendous flyover sweeping across its face.

The roundabout in front of us serves the Mersey Tunnel. This is affectionately known as the Old Tunnel, since it was built in the 1930s. The New Tunnel from the 1960s has gouged a hole across the districts either side of Scotland Road, about half a mile behind us along Byrom Street. The Old Tunnel was built between 1925 and 1934 and the

decoration was designed by Herbert Rowse, the architect of India Buildings and the Martin's Bank building on Water Street. His gorgeous Art Deco tunnel architecture is reminiscent of Ancient Egypt, but instead of winged suns there are winged wheels and muscular horses. The limestone kiosks are worth examining in some detail. When the roads were being improved in the 1970s, the little green tollbooths were sold off and George Harrison is supposed to have bought one for his Surrey garden.

Facing the roundabout is the **Old Haymarket**, a name revived for new apartments on Manchester Street, and

Steps outside the museum.

Railings and stonework , St John's Gardens.

St John's Gardens and Alfred Waterhouse's Pearl Assurance building on St John's Lane.

St John's Gardens, one of the few open spaces in the city centre. They are very well maintained with neat flowerbeds and trimmed grass, and in summer are busy at lunchtime with picnickers and children released from the solemnities of the Museum to eat their sandwiches and run off some energy. They fill the Gardens with their games and chatter, and run unheedingly around the statues.

The Gardens were originally the burial ground for St John's Church. The church was built in 1783 on what was still called the Great Heath, although a burial ground had been here for some time. After the Wellington Monument there is more quiet Napoleonic history here; on the back of the great semi-circular stone seat is a plaque to the French prisoners of war buried here between 1772 and 1803. St John's was designed in an unhappy Gothic style, and generally ridiculed for its ugliness and pretension; few mourned when the church was demolished in 1898 to clear the ground for the new Anglican Cathedral, which fortunately was never built. Instead the old burial ground was laid out as a public garden, and opened in 1904. It was intended to be Liverpool's open-air sculpture gallery, but was nicknamed 'the Stoneyard' almost immediately. St John's Gardens has been described as Liverpool's Valhalla, as the grounds are dotted with statues commemorating Liverpool's great men, famous in politics or social reform, designed by some of the leading sculptors of the time. The most imposing are the statue commemorating William Ewart Gladstone, with its mournful winged-and-helmeted figures of Justice and Truth, and the famous sculpture remembering the dead of the King's Regiment, with its relaxed, dignified bronze soldiers. There are smaller military

Queen Square, 1951. (LCC)

Queen Square, 2004.

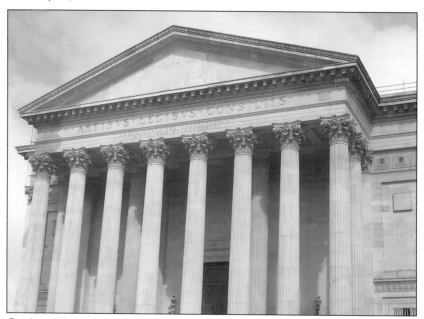

Evening sunlight on the southern porch of St George's Hall.

monuments to the city's dead from the Normandy campaign to Korea, and a plaque commemorating World Aids Day.

St John's Church has given its name to the Gardens, to the unlovely shopping precinct, and to the Lane running down the side towards the Tunnel. The imposing Gothic tower was built – perhaps inevitably – by Alfred Waterhouse as the Pearl Assurance Building, and has survived the massive upheavals of this area to become restaurants and an excellent pub, Dr Duncan's, which we drink in on the pubs walk. The pedestrianised road down the side leads us to Queen Square.

Queen Square is a new development. It sits on the footprint of an older Queen Square which was an extension of the huge St John's Markets which ran along Great Charlotte Street and sold fish, meat, vegetables and fruit. The tiny pattern of narrow streets surrounding old Queen Square was demolished in the 1960s for a development that was never built, and the area languished as a car park until it was redeveloped in the mid-1990s.

This whole area is unrecognisable from the urban landscape of the 1960s, but to their credit the developers have restored the street pattern with pedestrianised lanes, and once again Tryon Street cuts from St John's Lane to Hood Street and Great Charlotte Street runs from Roe Street to Whitechapel. The skyline is dominated by a huge hotel, and a five-storey car park, thoughtfully clad in brick to resemble the Victorian warehouses which once stood here. As a car park, it is invisible. Modern Queen Square is smartly cobbled and the little streets are lined with bars and restaurants. Ahead of us across the bus lanes of **Roe Street** is the ugly mass of the St John's Precinct and the solid red-brick Art Deco of the Royal Court, one of the city's top venues for pop and rock bands. The massive south portico of St George's Hall looms over us as we cross the road to the start of the walk at **Lime Street Station**.

The South Docks and the Overhead Railway

'The salt tides love her…'
Edmund Burke, *'Liverpool'*.

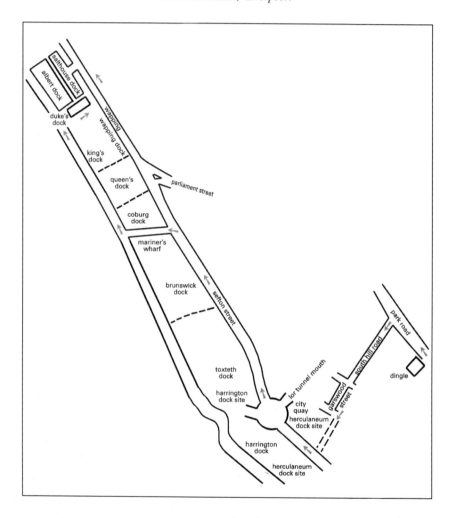

The Liverpool Overhead Railway at its peak ran from the Dingle in the south of the city to Seaforth in the north, a distance of some seven miles. The railway ran on a series of iron gantries some 30 feet above the roadway, and was an excellent way to see the boats and huge liners berthed in the busy Liverpool docks. It was the first electric elevated railway in the world and opened in 1893. Affectionately known as The Dockers' Umbrella, the name used by Paul Bolger as the title of his excellent book on the railway, in old photographs the Overhead has an industrial glamour; the rattle and clatter of heavy trains on iron gantries, the hoots of steam horns, the noise and bustle of the docks. The buildings seem to be made of grey dusty wood, and look simultaneously solid and fragile, modern and very old-fashioned.

By the 1950s the salt wind had taken its toll on the ironwork and some two million pounds was needed to restore it, a vast sum in those days. The decision was taken to close and in 1956 the Overhead Railway was demolished.

The railway was built on a framework of iron, which was simply cut from the streets and carted away. Very little survives along the dock roads and for that reason this is a walk through the landscape of the docks, the oldest industry in the city, in the vanished shadow of the Overhead Railway. Since the end of World War Two the docks have declined as an industry, a fact brought to public attention perhaps during the Dockers' Strike of the 1990s. Now much of the traditional work and jobs associated with the docks have gone, and the waterfront is seen by the city as a playground, a place for expensive apartment blocks looking out over empty water. But there are still stretches of historical interest; cobbles and railway lines, capstans and huge overgrown granite blocks that once formed the edges of docks. This is not a history of the docks, a list of dates and cargoes and tonnages, but a walk of landscapes and echoes, finding poetry in dereliction and beauty in rust.

Dingle Station, 926. *(LCC)*

This is a walk for hardcore urban explorers only, and is not suitable for children. There are very few toilet breaks or pubs, and only a handful of cafés, which cater mainly for the people who work on the docks.

There is nothing above ground to suggest that there was once a railway station in the Dingle. The site of the Overhead station is now a car showroom and garage, and the platforms and track bed underground are supposedly used for car storage. **Park Road** leads up the hill towards the highest point in Toxteth, past the Holy Land, a series of streets named after Old Testament figures, and recently featured in a Channel 4 TV series. They are a Victorian reminder that this land was first settled in the early 17th century by Puritans from the Midlands, before which it had never been farmed, never been lived on; it was part of the royal park of Toxteth, protected from agriculture or hunting by the grim Forest Laws. We turn left onto **South Hill Road**.

All this area was once terraced streets, but the city council has demolished many substandard or derelict properties and built attractive houses and bungalows more suited to modern living, with gardens and space to park a car off the road. On the far side of Beloe Street is a large open space used as a recreation ground, with fine views across the river to Ellesmere Port and the Welsh hills. Crossing Cockburn Street at the end of South Hill Road we come to **Garswood Street** leading down to **Grafton Street**. This is an area strangely popular with filmmakers; the Albert Finney film (and Liverpudlian cultural landmark) *Gumshoe* was partly filmed on the recreation ground at the end of Grafton Street, and both *The Liver Birds* and *Bread* were filmed on the steep streets tumbling down towards the river.

Below us is the site of the Herculaneum Dock, now a modern housing development. The dock took its name from the Herculaneum Pottery which flourished here between

City Quay housing development, a watery echo of the old Herculaneum Dock.

Cobbles at the Herculaneum Dock.

A supporting beam from the Overhead Railway.

Dock railway lines at Herculaneum.

1796 and 1841, the most famous pottery in the town. The dock opened in 1866 and was used for ship repair, and to ship oil, petrol, and resins, and the casemates built into the cliff were used to store dangerous or volatile substances. The dock closed in 1972 and was filled soon after.

There is a staircase of granite and sandstone to the left, at the very end of Grafton Street, which takes us down to ground level perhaps 100 feet below. The massive walls and balustrades of the staircase are very impressive, the more so for being hidden and not much used. Some of the cobbles and railway lines of the old dock are visible under drifts of leaves to the left of the path leading to **Riverside Drive**.

The Overhead Railway emerged from the Dingle Tunnel above the health club 200 yards along the road to our right. The tunnel mouth can clearly be seen from the road, and up close it assumes the immensity and dignity of a Roman ruin; the names of engineers and company directors are chiselled deeply into its clean face, and have stared out across the river for over 100 years. The wall between the car park and the union offices next door is a Victorian survivor, and still has some of the huge iron girders used to support the railway embedded in it. The roundabout marks roughly the site of the old Herculaneum Station, later a carriage shed when the extension to the Dingle was dug in 1896.

The southern docks have seen huge amounts of investment, sparked by the International Garden Festival of 1984. From here to the Pier Head, they have been converted to modern use. Large apartment blocks have been built, the marina developed, businesses attracted to the area. The cost of riverside accommodation means that it is out of reach for many local people, and the apartment blocks have something of a ghetto air about them, with prominent security and electric fences; on **Sefton Street**, which runs like a spine from Herculaneum Dock to Parliament Street, modern show rooms for luxury cars have replaced the old dock businesses.

Tunnel for the Overhead Railway.

Cobbles at Harrington Dock.

Two views of the entrance to Herculaneum Dock.

Toxteth Dock from the Horsfall Street ramp, 2004.

It is worth crossing the road here to see **Harrington Dock**, opened in the 1880s, which was regenerated a century later. The dock was filled in and the old brick warehouses were smartened up as small business units and workshops. Very little attention was paid to the landscaping at this end of the dock complex, and the old entrance to Herculaneum and Herrington Docks can clearly be seen next to the Chinese restaurant. The curve of the huge dock wall can be seen just off the roundabout, as well as prominent dock 'furniture' like bollards and capstans, warehouse floors of heavy granite setts, and forgotten railway lines embedded in cobbles and weeds. We can either walk through the business park, where there are occasional pieces of dock 'furniture', or return to **Sefton Street**. Either way we head into the city centre, towards the Pier Head.

The gigantic ramp in front of the modern Brunswick Station was built in 1866 to enable Horsfall Street to leapfrog the railway and reach Sefton Street. It has worn stone steps and gently decaying ironwork, and good views over the railway and the docks below. This was once a very industrial area, with the huge Mersey Forge employing hundreds of people on three yards around Horsfall and Grafton Streets until the early 20th century.

Toxteth Dock was created in the 1880s, but it too has been filled in and turned into a small business park. The stubby tower has been kept mainly as a clock tower and is a strong and handsome feature in an area largely devoid of architectural attraction. Sefton Street at this point has been landscaped with a small avenue of trees on reclaimed cobbles, which unfortunately cannot compete with ugly, bleached red crash barriers from the 1980s or the old sandstone wall behind them. The empty ground behind the wall was once part of the Brunswick Goods Yard. The Overhead Railway ran along Sefton Street at this point and Toxteth Dock Station stood at the bottom of Park Street, but with

relatively little at ground level, nothing has survived. The Customs Depot and the tower of the old engine house have survived on the new round-about, and have happily found new lives as offices for a charity.

Next to Harry Ramsden's is a naval establishment, HMS *Eaglet*, which opened in the late 1990s. Beyond the naval base Sefton Street has been redeveloped into a maritime suburb,

Modern landscaping on Sefton Street.

Vent on the Dock Road.

with houses and gardens on the site of the warehouses for Brunswick Dock, but there are long stretches of old dock wall here. The roundabout is new, built when the roads were put through the old docks. The anchor swinging heavily in the centre is one of a number of redundant objects reused as decoration; all along the docks anchors, buoys, and bollards have been reused, but they blend in too well and become invisible sculpture. This anchor is more successful than most, but it is still marooned as surely as Robinson Crusoe. The car showrooms opposite stand on the site of the old

Victorian pipework on the Dock Road.

Brunswick Dock Wall.

Brunswick Goods Station, a huge network of railway lines ultimately connecting the south docks with the rest of the country.

Brunswick Dock was the first to be built by Jesse Hartley, when he became superintendent of the docks in 1825. It was designed for the timber trade, and had an Overhead Station near the foot of Hill Street, but here too nothing survives. The dock is now part of the Liverpool Marina.

The Liverpool Watersport Centre is a success story of the regeneration of the south docks. The smart floating clubhouse on **Mariner's Wharf** has won architectural acclaim, and there are many pleasure boats moored in the old docks of Brunswick and Coburg, with their echoes of 19th-century royal marriages. At weekends Coburg Dock is used by water sports enthusiasts, and is full of canoeists and wind surfers.

The old Brunswick dockyard on the river has been cleared and a small village of new apartment houses built. They are solid, rather squat buildings, crouched against the wind and salt; but they are surrounded by water and there is the sound of rope tapping on mast like Blind Pew heading towards the Admiral Benbow, and the gentle, mournful ringing of distant ship's bells.

The Customs & Excise Service has a new building straddling the graving dock for the old Queen's Dock, with an impressive semi-circular wall heavily and attractively decorated to

Railway track and new planting at Queen's Dock.

commemorate the business and old trades of the docks. **Queen's Dock**, opened in 1795, was used for the importing of tobacco, as well as palm oil, hides and coffee and the export of salt and coal. **King's Dock** is now a wasteland. It was built in 1789 and imported and exported many of the same goods as Queen's Dock, trading chiefly with America and the Baltic countries, a commerce remembered in the Baltic Fleet, one of the last pubs on the dock road. It was unsuitable for the larger vessels of the later 20th century and was filled in the 1980s, since when it has been indifferently used as a car park. (But perhaps because of this much of the ground level material has survived; cobbles, iron runners, stone floors.) It is shameful that the city cannot find an imaginative use for this huge site; in the summer pop concerts are held here, and some white apartments have been built near **Duke's Dock**, but the rest of the King's Dock is a great empty space.

Sefton Street has more old warehouses than anywhere else on the southern docks and even one old dockside pub. Most of the warehouse buildings are still used for storage and transport, although the goods are carried by road now, and one has been converted into a landlocked boat building yard, manufacturing narrowboats. At Parliament Street the dock road becomes Chaloner Street, before becoming Wapping.

Nothing survives of the Overhead between these docks and the Pier Head, the break on our walk. There was an aerial station for Wapping Dock at the foot of Blundell Street, and a few iron columns which once supported the Overhead Railway have been retained in the massive cyclopean wall of **Wapping Dock**. In 1796 William Moss wrote that the large warehouses on Wapping were chiefly used for storing corn, and on his walk he found 'roperies, anchor smithies, block-makers, sail-makers, and every business connected with the naval department, in great abundance, together with a number of public houses...' Behind the modern sculpture, the *Superlambanana*, one of these businesses survives; Joseph Lamb have been fitting ships since the late 18th century and still have a depot and offices on a fragment of Hurst Street. There were also chandlers, coopers, dry salters and a timber yard on the river side of Wapping, which were cleared for the building of Wapping Dock and Basin in the 1850s. The artist John Atkinson

Jessie Hartley's 'Mediaeval' dock buildings at Wapping.

The Overhead Railway and the Pier Head, photographed from Brunswick Street in 1948.

Ironwork nameplate for the Overhead Railway.

Grimshaw painted *Liverpool from Wapping* in 1875 and *Liverpool Quay by Moonlight* in 1887, both of this area; his smoky golden views of a dock road busy with horse-drawn carriages are immensely popular in Liverpool, and available in every print shop.

We are now at the **Albert Dock/Pier Head**, an area explored in detail in the Pier Head walk. There were three stations here on the Overhead; Custom House Station stood on

Strand Street in front of the gigantic Customs House, James Street had a station at its junction with the Strand, and Pier Head Station, the busiest on the line, stood in front of the Liver Buildings. All have now vanished without trace.

This first stretch of the walk ends here, with plenty of pubs and eating places in the Albert Dock and the streets up towards the Town Hall. The Maritime Museum has an excellent display of ceramics from the Herculaneum Pottery, and an informative exhibition on the industry in Liverpool.

Overhead Railway girder at Wapping

Dock Road near Canning Place, 1958. *(LCC)*

Demolition of the Overhead Railway, 1958. *(LCC)*

WALK 8

The North Docks
and the Overhead Railway

'Old Liverpool of gutters, weeds, capstan full strength and old men who call you "Bud"…'
Liverpool writer Jeff Young

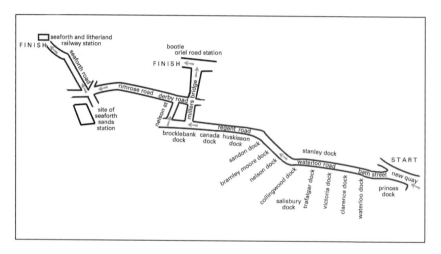

This is a companion walk to the exploration of the southern docks, and explores the old Overhead Railway route north from the Pier Head to Seaforth. It is not a history of the docks but an exploration of landscape and surviving architecture. It is essentially a walk along the long dock road, here called Waterloo Road and Regent Road, but it is worth exploring the narrow streets on the landward side, especially at the beginning of the walk, as many still have the tall, thin warehouses which have been cleared from much of the old city centre. This northern dock road is a long way from the coffee shops of new Liverpool; it is a part of the city rich in history and architecture, but be warned – it can make for bleak walking. There are very few refreshment stops; there are a few cafés that cater for the dock workers, but they are few and far between. It is a noisy and dirty walk for urban exploration enthusiasts only, and is not suitable for children.

This seems an older part of the city, haunted by lost jobs and old trades, dockers' jokes and nicknames. It is a strange working landscape bigger than it needs to be, totally unlike anywhere else in the city. There are abandoned gateposts like lost Roman columns, and

A water fountain on the Dock Road north of the Pier Head.

grand dock gateways like the entrance to Greek temples. There are iron drinking fountains, set into the vast granite walls like delicate Baroque stoups, and isolated streets of soot-bricked warehouses, ropes or cables banging aimlessly in the wind. Huge lorries wait patiently outside Victorian warehouses with tiny barred windows. The road itself is always busy, with traffic using it to avoid the traffic lights of Derby Road, but there are no people.

The walk begins on the windy expanse of **New Quay**, which was a new waterfront laid out in the early 18th century. It becomes **Bath Street**, which remembers a number of elegant salt-and-fresh-water establishments which stood here, a reminder that this stretch of shoreline was once popular as a bathing resort. The old brick wall to our left was to protect Prince's Dock, the first of the northern docks, built in 1821. It closed in 1981 and was partially filled in during 1999–2000. The old Riverside Station was also demolished; thousands of people passed through here to emigrate to the New World, and it has been said many times that this was their last view of Britain or even Europe. The site has been partially developed as an hotel and the Seacat terminal, taking passengers to Ireland from where the Irish once sailed to America. There are also government offices and banks here, and the car park behind the wall is heavily monitored. It is worth braving the guards, however, for the wall has huge iron supports for the Overhead, and the cobbled floor still has the railway lines for the dock.

At the entrance to **Prince's Dock** car parks stood Prince's Dock Station, the first Overhead station north of the Pier Head, but a roundabout there now controls the traffic

Prince's Dock landing stage, 1919. *(LCC)*

Cobbles and rails in Prince's Dock.   LOR supporting beams.

to and from the new offices and banks on the waterfront. There were nine stations between the Pier Head and Seaforth, where the Overhead connected with the line to Southport at the Seaforth & Litherland Station, and as with the southern stations, very little remains of them now.

Waterloo Dock opened in 1834, initially to ease the pressure on Prince's Dock, and was used largely for grain and corn. The huge warehouse, with its solid stone arcades and tall brick walls, was in use until the 1980s when it was turned into apartments. North of the Pier Head the landscape is very different from the micro-businesses and modern homes on the old southern docks. Perhaps in five or ten years these northern docks will have been regenerated as completely as the docks south of the Pier Head, but at the time of writing the regeneration stretches no further than the apartments on Waterloo Dock. An older dock road emerges untouched by the 1990s or even the 1980s; a thin wire fence separates the BMWs and Audis in the car park from the windswept container depot beyond it.

North of Waterloo Dock the road opens out, as the depot on the left gives way to the empty field of **Clarence Dock**. The streets on the right still have many of their old warehouses, occupied now by the new dock businesses of scrap iron, haulage, printing and car repair shops, replacing the older ones of marine engineers, boat building and ships' suppliers. There are tiny fragments of dock road frontage, pubs boarded solid, aloof empty warehouses. Lascar House was an old pub, then a car business, now boarded solid and silently remembering the Malay seamen who once came here.

Clarence Dock opened on an isolated site in 1830, as it was designed to receive steam

Waterloo Dock.

ships with the accompanying danger of sparks, but it was rapidly surrounded; Trafalgar and Victoria were built in the late 1830s and a great swathe was built by Jesse Hartley in the 1840s. Salisbury, Collingwood, Stanley, Nelson and Bramley-Moore Docks were all laid out at the same time, between 1844 and 1848, in a mammoth undertaking that employed 4,000 men. All have the distinctive 'cyclopean' walling beloved of Jesse Hartley, a wall which stretches for miles along the dock roads, with deep, crisply carved name-plates. Today only Clarence has any life to it, as its graving docks are still used for the repair of small

Victorian warehouse near Clarence Dock.

Lascar House, a former pub, now closed.

vessels, and it still has the bustle of a small shipyard. Clarence Dock was later the site of a power station, but that too has gone and only birds visit the large empty field it has left behind. Yet a small plaque commemorates the fact that for many years the Dock was the point of arrival for tens of thousands of Irish people who came to Liverpool after the Famine, many of whom settled in Vauxhall and found work on the docks.

Clarence Dock Station stood above the ground near Stanley Dock, which is the only dock in the system built on the landward side of the road. There is a cousin of the Albert Dock here, obviously Jesse Hartley's design, but abandoned and empty. It is dwarfed by the Stanley Dock Tobacco Warehouse, a giant of a building, supposedly big enough to store St George's Hall. This monster was built in 1900 and was the biggest warehouse in the world. Now it is empty, although it is possible that it will be developed into flats or bars. This is the most attractive stretch of the dock road; the iron bridge with its blue wooden operating rooms, the docks behind and in front, and the powerful sentinel clock

Stanley Dock.

tower of **Salisbury Dock**, still imposing a century and a half after being built.

Nelson Dock had a station on the Overhead, but nothing survives of the railway along this stretch apart from some great iron beams, buried in the walls. **Bramley-Moore Dock** was named after the Chairman of the Dock Committee and Mayor of Liverpool and had its own high-level railway system linking it to

Tobacco warehouse at Stanley Dock.

Dock traffic near Stanley Dock, 1956.

The Victoria Tower at Salisbury Dock.

Dock Gate Wheel.

the Lancashire & Yorkshire Railway. The huge terracotta tower can still be seen, although most of the dock now seems to be used by sand and stone merchants. **Sandon Dock** is now home to the city's vast modern sewage treatment plant. The dock opened in 1851 and still has its delicate terracotta gatehouse. There is a modern business park opposite, made a little bleached and shabby by the salt and the wind, the legacy of the sea; a huge sugar silo like an aircraft hangar, an electricity substation called Molasses. It feels American here; pipes crossing the road, huge vats and silos, like the dockland back streets of a nameless city, the scene of a car chase or a clandestine meeting. It smells of sugar, salt, oil, with occasional blasts of hot café air, Cornish pasties and coffee. There is thick mud on the road, and the endless noise of heavy lorries bouncing on the smoothly uneven surface.

And further out the docks seem busier. There are ships being repaired, lorries unloading containers, more activity. The docks here are bigger, and so have survived longer; often it was their size that made them unworkable. **Huskisson Dock** opened in

Molasses sub-station.

Stone and brick walls on Regent Road.

Abandoned ironwork.

Cyclopean stone.

Fulton Street warehouses.

The Dominion.

1852, named after the unlucky MP killed by the *Rocket*, Canada Dock in 1859, with its pub the Dominion and the famous lumberjack and his dog standing on top. Both had Overhead stations, but nothing is left of the railway here.

The water, invisible from the road but never far away, suddenly appears; acres of deep, green water, silent cold walls, empty and oily or whipped up angrily on cold January afternoons to a blue-green, with flicks of white spume. Ships from Panama, Malta, Bratislava, Liberia. Flashes of arc welding as hulls are repaired, as cars are driven onto a huge ferry in **Brocklebank Dock**. There are great coils of cable and spools of rope, signs of industry. There are solid architectural survivors, the Atlantic pub, the Langton Castle, Harland & Wolff's engineering works. But here as elsewhere there are also rusting iron railway tracks running into empty yards across overgrown cobbles. The road is busy but

Abstract cobbles.

there are pavements never used, cobbles still solid beneath mud becoming soil. The wind seems fiercer here, colder, the noise of the wind blowing thin cable, tattered ropes.

The old road along the docks is barred now at **Nelson Street**. Once the Overhead ran on, passing through Alexandra and Gladstone Dock stations before turning through Seaforth Sands and meeting the main Southport railway line at Seaforth Station. Now a great swathe of the docks has been revitalised as the Liverpool Freeport, which is supposed to handle more cargo and make more money than the old docks ever did.

The Dominion Lumberjack.

Taking the busy **Miller's Bridge** road, we cross Derby Road and can catch a train at **Oriel Road Station** in Bootle, which will take us back into Liverpool. The walk can be extended and walked along **Derby Road** and **Rimrose Road**, to the **Regent Road** junction where Seaforth Sands station once stood, suggesting salt air and clean open spaces after the industry of the docks. Taking **Seaforth Road** on our right we can pass through pretty Seaforth village to the railway station, where once the Overhead met the Southport trains, and from there catch a train to the city centre.

A door to Harland and Wolff's engineering works.

Allerton Parkland

This is a family walk through some quiet stretches of suburban Liverpool, across Allerton Golf Course and up into Woolton, and can be extended to cover an exploration of Camp Hill. It will take between an hour and a half and two hours, and there are no steep hills or gradients. There are plenty of opportunities for picnics and café breaks, and the walk finishes in Woolton, with plenty of restaurants and good pubs, and easy transport links with the city centre. I have always thought of this as an autumnal walk; there are many beech trees on the walk, which look their best at this time of year and I have often found large shaggy ink cap mushrooms and ceps in the woods. Much of the walk is through woodland and the paths can be muddy, so care should be taken in wet weather.

Allerton was farmland until the middle years of the 19th century, when Liverpool's rich began to build large country estates here, and it is through these , now owned by the city, that the walk takes us. There is something of a Roman feel to these estates, now turned into golf courses or public parks; their attempts at classical landscaping are overgrown and their homes are demolished or turned into offices, leaving only lonely obelisks, the shells of Italianate buildings, or giant broken columns buried in the woods.

The walk starts at **Allerton Library**, on **Allerton Road**. The library was built between 1964 and 1965, and with its large windows and neat cobbles, it still looks modern today. This is the quiet end of Allerton Road; the traffic swings past the library, and Allerton Road meanders off into the trees in front of us. The police and fire stations on the right were built in the early 20th century, and are very attractive neo-Georgian buildings in deep red brick. This is a quietly smart district, with large semi-detached houses and trees in well-kept grounds. The streets are quiet

The imposing entrance into Calderstones Park.

and peaceful. As the last house ends on the right hand side, the view opens up across the Territorial Army grounds to the church of St Michael and St James on Mossley Hill.

The large Victorian church in front of us is All Hallows', Allerton. It was built in 1876 by John Bibby to commemorate his wife, Fanny Hartley, the daughter of Jesse Hartley, the great dock builder. The churchyard supposedly has a Glastonbury thorn in it, but is chiefly famous for the fact that all but one of its windows are by Edward Burne-Jones. We follow the road to the left of the church and turn right at the small crossroads. This is **Harthill Road**,

Harthill Lodge.

Harthill Spring.

named after John Bibby's estate, Harthill, which is on the right at the top of the hill. Nothing survives of the buildings, although the pretty Gothic lodge survives as a private house and a second (classical) lodge still stands on Calderstones Road. The grounds have long been incorporated into Calderstones Park and served as nursery and workshops for the parks and gardens department of the Corporation. On our left is the modern Calderstones Community School, which covers the sites of two Victorian mansions, Hartfield and Quarry Bank. For many years it was known as Quarrybank High School. An early incarnation of the Beatles was called the Quarrymen, a loose collaboration of musicians and friends orbiting John Lennon, the school's most famous ex-pupil.

At the junction with Calderstones Road we turn sharp right into **Calderstones Park**, through the imposing entrance that was once the main entrance to Harthill. The giant Atlantes statues were originally positioned on Brown's Buildings, designed by James Picton, and they are offset well by the graceful figures of the four seasons. The broad path ahead of us cuts across what was once the Harthill estate, with the classical lodge visible on the left.

In later life the Harthill estate housed the Liverpool Botanic Gardens, the legacy of William Roscoe. They were opened in September 1964 by Sir George Taylor, the Director of Kew, and replaced an earlier garden on Edge Lane, which was destroyed in 1940. To the city's shame the Botanic Gardens were decommissioned in the 1980s, and all that survives now is a large stone on the right hand side of the path, in front of a rather shabby pavilion with scratched plastic windows. Yet inside are the Calder Stones, the Stone Age tomb that gives the Park and district its name. The original site was at the entrance to the Park on Menlove Avenue, and for many centuries the Stones marked one of the boundaries between Allerton and Wavertree. The burial mound was excavated in the 18th century, and some earthenware burial jars were found. But there was no gold or great treasure, so the jars were stored in a barn where they were played with by local

Calderstones Park, 2004.

The Japanese Garden, Calderstones Park, 2004.

children, and eventually broken and the contents dispersed. And the shabby treatment of the Calder Stones continues today; the city should be proud of its oldest man-made structure and display the Stones properly, instead of hiding them away in an ugly plastic shed.

The main path leads us in a gentle curve through the park, with the original Calderstone house visible on the left, to the junction with **Yew Tree Lane** and the next stage of the walk. Yet there is much to see here in this park. There are safe playgrounds, lots of space for children to run about, as well as interesting things for adults. Past the old Botanic Gardens the path enters a grove of very tall old trees, and forms a crossroads with a path from Allerton Road that leads to the old house. To our right are the gates from Bidston Court, which have stood here since 1974; their elegant iron curls and swirls almost disappear into the leaves, yet at dusk on a winter's evening they mirror the bare branches of the tall trees.

To our left the path leads us past the careful lawns and deep flowerbeds of the old house's original private gardens, the elegant Victorian hot houses with their collections of cacti and desert plants, and two of the city's hidden gardens, the Old English Garden and the beautiful Japanese Garden. Both are best seen out of school holidays, as for some reason both are popular with rowdy boys; but both are quiet and secluded places, a hidden corner to lose an hour in a book or just to admire the planting. Liverpool has many of these hidden corners outside the city centre.

Calderstones Park, 2004

In front of us is Calderstone, the 'Mansion House', built in a simple Neo-classical style. The house is now private offices for the city council, but it also has a cheerful café and toilets.

The Park also has Liverpool's oldest tree, the Allerton Oak. The broad path to the left leads past the stables and the old outdoor theatre to the site of the Calder Stones outside the Park, but from it a path on the right hand side leads past flower beds and the ponies' gravestone (a large weathered sandstone gravestone, marking the burial place of ponies mourned by the family in the 1820s) to the twisted branches and fat trunk of the oldest tree in the city. Huge iron crutches hold up the tree and its heart has gone, yet each spring new growth appears, and each autumn new acorns fall. And occasionally people still tie ribbons and charms to the great tree, as perhaps they have done self-consciously for hundreds of years.

From the front of the house the walk continues across the little stone bridge over one of the few ha-has in the city. These were hidden ditches to enable the view across pasture to be enjoyed without the animals trampling the grass in front of the house. To our right is a safe children's playground, named after Linda McCartney, a reminder that both Paul McCartney and John Lennon grew up near here and would have known the Park well. Across the big field is the lake, which attracts fishermen and many types of birds, especially geese, ducks and more unusual species such as coot and moorhen. The banks have been recently landscaped to help both the birds and the anglers. Rejoining the main pathway through the park we pass the lake on our left and a small car park on the right, handy for visitors to the new tennis tournament held in Calderstones Park every summer.

Through the imposing gateposts is **Yew Tree Lane**, which can be a busy road, and a noisy racetrack after the quiet of the park. Opposite is a small footpath that leads in a dead straight line up the slight hill towards the golf course.

The bustle of Yew Tree Lane is quickly lost, and the mood becomes quieter, more rural; the old sandstone walls and trees overhead make the city seem a long way away, and in late summer the bushes in the field to our left are full of blackberries. The path leads past the fields to new woodland at the top, managed by Liverpool John Moores University on the grounds of an old house called Dowsefield. The path through the woods is very pleasant on dry days, but muddy and slippery after rain; if it is wet, stay on the tarmac path. The Dowsefield path joins the golf course boundary path at the top, so turn right to rejoin the main route. This is as rural as urban Liverpool gets; all around us now are fields, woods, or the tall trees and bushes surrounding the open greens of the municipal golf course. We follow the path round the sandstone wall to the right, and through the new path to emerge near the first hole of **Allerton Golf Course**. The golf course sits at the top of a hill, in the grounds of a house simply called Allerton or Allerton Manor, built for the merchant Jacob Fletcher in 1815 by Thomas Harrison, the architect of the Lyceum Post Office on Bold Street.

We follow the road to the left, through the old stables and sandstone outbuildings of

Allerton Golf Course, 1934, showing Allerton Manor through the trees. *(LCC)*

Allerton Manor today.

the house. These imposing buildings are now the offices and bar of the golf course. All that survives of the house are the walls, now gently and beautifully decaying; the putting lawns in front are immaculate, but there are trees and bushes growing in what were drawing rooms, dining rooms. A long colonnade survives and a grand doorway, but the building is now only half a shell. And yet recent clearing of wooden sheds and containers has tidied the landscape, and the shape of the house seems clearer. Directly in front of the colonnade is an obelisk, supposedly exactly eight miles from the old measuring point at the Exchange behind the town hall, and once the elegant terminus of an avenue of beeches from Allerton Hall.

Following the road to the left of the obelisk, we can see across the Mersey and the Wirral to the distant Welsh mountains. The path leads through thick rhododendron woods to the golf course, which cleverly takes the grassland and plantations of trees

Allerton Manor and the obelisk.

The colonnade of Allerton Manor.

surrounding the old house and transforms them into fairways and greens, so that the golf is played around ancient beeches and stands of birch trees.

Great care must be taken here; the path leads across the golf course proper to the road in the tall trees opposite, but it crosses a fairway, and golf balls can be travelling at very high speeds.

Once in the trees, a lost road appears. To our right, the road leads past the golf course to Allerton Road. To our left it dips downhill to join Menlove Avenue at Woolton village, and straight ahead it leads to Woolton Road opposite Camp Hill and Allerton Hall. Perhaps once all the roads around here looked like this, muddy farm tracks between the high sandstone walls of the local estates. On the right, the finest survivor of these great Victorian estates is well worth a small detour. This is Allerton Priory, built between 1867 and 1870 by Alfred Waterhouse for a colliery owner, John Grant Morris. It is not Waterhouse's best work, but after years of different uses and indifferent owners it has been renovated as apartments and the fine Gothic detailing is as crisp and clean as when it was first built.

The large green gates to our left lead us into the grounds of **Allerton Tower**, which was built for the Earle family in 1847 by Harvey Lonsdale Elmes, the young architect of St George's Hall. Very little survives of the house today, but the solid brick classicism of the stable block is intact and the pretty lodge survives on the Woolton Road entrance. The stable block is used as an outdoor pursuits centre by the city council and sometimes there are canoes on the high banks under the trees, as if left by a high tide.

The columns from the old Church for the Blind, buried in ivy on Camp Hill.

Turning left past the old stable block (walking across what was once the house itself) the Orangery appears on our left. This is all that survives of the old house, and it is as melancholy as only a derelict building of such aristocratic uselessness can be. The paint peeling from its plaster, the arches crumbling, the roof fallen away, it is nevertheless a very beautiful building, and one of my favourite places in the whole city. There is never anybody here; this is a lost park, a hidden landscape, and with the cedar trees against the blue sky on a hot day, the architect's vision of an Italian landscape is realised. It is made more surprising by the crisp hedges and careful landscaping maintained by the city council; this gives it an Alice-In-Wonderland quality, a slight madness. Turning left at the columned entrance steps to the Orangery, we are in another of the city's hidden gardens. Visible through the gate to our left is the magnificent stable block, imposingly classical, sturdy red brick with sandstone dressings and a vast cobbled yard. The gardens to our right are protected by trees, hedges and a fine brick wall, and in high summer are a riot of colourful bedding plants. It has a *gingko biloba*, a Maidenhair Tree, a genus older than the dinosaurs, older than insects; it has an arbour of roses, a long lawn, simple paths. It is one of the best of the city's hidden gardens, and in all my visits I have never seen anybody else here.

Returning to the long walk under the arbour at the bottom of the garden, the path begins to climb past huge stone pines and yews, and comes out onto **Menlove Avenue**. A bus to the city centre can be caught at the bus stop to our right. Ahead of us lies **Woolton**, the best country village in the city, which has many good pubs, cafés, and restaurants.

The walk can be extended by exploring Camp Hill and Woolton Woods, which are across the leafy dual carriageway to our right and up the slight hill. Woolton Woods has a crown of gigantic trees and a great slope leading to Hillfoot Avenue. From the top, the view stretches to Speke and the airport and across Allerton Tower and Clarke's Gardens, a landscape of trees uninterrupted by buildings. There is a short route around the top of the hill that passes the hidden walled garden, which is well-maintained and full of colour in the summer. Camp Hill is smaller and quieter, with a sunken garden and the giant columns from the Church for the Blind on Hotham Street buried under ivy, just off the main path.

WALK 10

Lost Docks
and the Pier Head

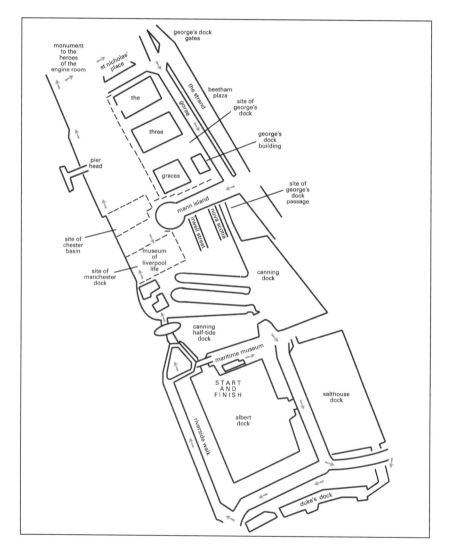

Liverpool begins and ends at the river. It was the river and the sea that gave the city its special grit and character, and provided its young men with work. Generations of Liverpudlians went to sea, and many of the city's teachers, financial advisers, driving instructors and artists now in their early 60s started their working lives on merchant ships or liners sailing to New Westminster or Rio de Janeiro. The docks employed not only hundreds of dockers to load and unload the cargoes, but also ships' outfitters like sail makers, joiners, painters, glaziers, metalworkers and riveters.

This is a walk around the heart of the old docks system, the Pier Head. There is an imperial confidence and bustle here, with huge buildings and the roar of the traffic, but there is also a sombre poetry of sadness and departure, of emigrants leaving and the creaking slave ships returning to George's Dock laden with goods from America. Today much of the business and life have left the river altogether. Old men sit at the Pier Head feeding the pigeons or staring out to sea, perhaps to remember old voyages or comrades, and with the breezy smell of salt water and its memorials the Pier Head is a quiet and meditative place. The area is best explored on a misty day, a rainy day, when the visitors are all in the shops of the Albert Dock and the river slops mournfully at the landing stage, and all we can hear are the old river sounds of faint bells and the cry of the gulls.

The best way to explore this area is to start and finish at the **Albert Dock**, known affectionately as *the* Dock. This impressive collection of warehouses, the largest collection of Grade I listed buildings in the country, was built by Jesse Hartley and opened by Prince Albert in 1846. They cannot be said to be pretty; they are strong,

Albert Dock and the Anglican Cathedral.

masculine buildings, sleeves rolled up and muscles bulging, and Liverpool's beloved classical architecture is here stripped down to its essentials of massive Tuscan columns and heavy round arches. Famously, they were rescued from dereliction in the 1980s and converted to apartments and shops, and the Dock also houses the superb **Maritime Museum** and Tate Liverpool, the gallery's northern outpost. But nothing is made of the water; the Dock is empty of ships apart from once a year during the Mersey River Festival, when it is alive with boats as it was meant to be, large vessels in the half-tide dock and smaller ones in the Albert and the Salthouse Docks. The Albert Dock has smart bars and fashionable restaurants, but many of the shops are second-rate, selling sweets and cheap toys, and not even the big attractions can save the visitors from thinking 'Is that it, is this all there is?'

Between Albert Dock and the traffic lanes of the Strand is **Salthouse Dock**. It is older than Albert, and is the oldest complete dock in the system. It was built to serve the salt works, then one of the most important industries in the town, and opened as South Dock in 1753. The dock sent ships to Ireland and Scotland, and they returned with great cargoes of granite, pickled herrings, hides, and beer. The south gable of the transit shed

across the water has been rebuilt, and near the car park is a small garden for the blind and disabled, with water trickling over a granite bollard and plants chosen for their strong texture or smell.

Duke's Dock was the only private dock in the system, built for the Duke of Bridgewater's cotton and grain boats in 1773. It had an early warehouse which arched over the water, allowing boats to be unloaded under cover. This was regrettably demolished in the 1960s, as the south docks began to close. Duke's Dock today is quiet and overlooked, with cold, clean, green-black water, and some fine stonework. It is a popular if illegal place for boys to swim in hot weather. Beyond this is the flat wilderness of the King's Dock, which we bemoaned on the Overhead Railway walk.

At the riverward side of the Albert Dock is our first glimpse of the river, wide and empty, and a view across to the towers and church spires of Birkenhead and up towards the distant Irish Sea. The Riverside Walk here connects the city centre with Garston, and Liverpool-born artist Tony Cragg has created a strong iron and stone sculpture for this green space called *Raleigh*, suggestive of quaysides and ships' horns, a name echoing with the Americas of the 1500s and adventurous modern youngsters.

Jesse Hartley was responsible for the development of the whole dock system for 40 years, and his attention to the smallest detail is shown in the watch-houses on the quay here, heavy roofs and thick walls to protect the dock staff from the weather roaring in from the Irish Sea. The edges of the granite are still crisp, the joints still good. Here they are maintained and looked after, but elsewhere on the docks his 'cyclopean' stonework is still in as good a condition.

Iron and stone sculpture *Raleigh*, by Tony Cragg.

The depths of Canning Dock.

The path leads us over the bridge and to the entrance to the **Canning Half-Tide Dock**, where the Maritime Museum has bigger exhibits and the tall ships stay when they are in Liverpool. Canning Dock was developed from the tidal basin of the Old Dock, and some of its stone walls date back to 1737. To the right is one of the entrances to the **Museum of Liverpool Life**, a small but very interesting museum. The mood in the Museum is like listening to the hubbub in a Liverpool pub; only gradually does it dawn that all the tales are a part of the one story. There is a room from the old Sailor's Home, a *Crucifixion* by Stuart Sutcliffe, one of the crush barriers from the Kop, a Ford Anglia from the car plant in Halewood. The crisp old Pilotage building, red brick and hard

Leftover railway lines in Canning Dock.

terracotta dated 1883, is also part of the Museum. It has a plaque remembering over one million Irish people who left Liverpool between 1845 and 1852, and a small sculpture commemorates the hundreds of thousands of European emigrants who left through Liverpool in the late 19th and early 20th century.

Already we can see the most famous waterfront in the world appearing ahead of us, but on the sea wall to our left is the

Pier Head shelter, 1901. *(LCC)*

Pier Head from the air, 1907. *(LCC)*

bricked up entrance to **Manchester Dock**, a reminder that this 'land' has been built and reclaimed many times. The giant buildings of the **Pier Head** are built over a pattern of outdated docks; Manchester Dock was built in 1785 to cater for the Mersey 'flats', local trading vessels with flattened hulls to navigate the shallower river waters, and Chester Basin was a tiny dock built in 1795 for boats serving the new canal from Ellesmere Port to Chester. Both docks had become too small by the end of the 19th century and were filled between 1928 and 1936 by rubble from the new Mersey road tunnel. The biggest of these buried docks was George's Dock, which was connected to Canning Dock by a narrow cut called George's Dock Passage, the stump of which can be seen behind Mann Island. George's Dock opened in 1771 as Liverpool was beginning to trade on a world scale, and slave ships sailed from here to West Africa, the West Indies and North America. In all the monuments on the Pier Head there is nothing remembering the victims of slavery, but the dock is recalled in local street names and the official name of the Pier Head sea wall, George's Parade.

The Pier Head is a creation of the 20th century, and its three dominant buildings – the Three Graces – form the most famous landscape in the city, instantly recognisable all over the world. From the right they are the Port of Liverpool Building, built in 1907 as the head offices of the Mersey Docks & Harbour Board, the Cunard Building, built between 1913 and 1916 for the steamship company, and the Liver Building, the most famous of them all, built between 1908 and 1911 as the headquarters of the Royal Liver Friendly Society. They dominate the whole waterfront and the city behind. All are very different architecturally: the Port of Liverpool Building is confidently, elaborately Baroque, the Cunard Building is designed along the lines of a vast *palazzo* with suitable

The Three Graces and the docks of the Maritime Museum.

Detail of the Liver Building.

American overtones, and the Liver Building seems unique, with an eclectic, defensive solidity, and hints of Art Nouveau and the Baroque. They look their best seen from the river, and the easiest and cheapest way to do this is to take a trip on the ferries. The Mersey Ferries have been taking travellers and commuters to and from the Cheshire shore of Birkenhead for 600 years, and were started by the monks of Stanlawe Abbey who rowed across the river between their lands. Today this is the best way to feel the swell and majesty of the river, as the large heavy ferryboats plough through the water to reach Woodside. The old river is still alive beneath these boats; the salty, oily smell of the Mersey air, the wrenching creak of the ropes, the shouts of the crew as the boats near the landing stage. Many of the famous pictures of the city were taken from the Birkenhead shore, to capture the racing clouds and huge skies over the Three Graces and the cathedrals behind.

For many years the Pier Head was the terminus of many of the city's bus and tram routes, but today the space is pedestrianised with elegant cobbled floors and wide grassed

Two views of the Port of Liverpool building.

The memorial to U-Boat hunter Johnny Walker.

spaces. There are many memorials here and most commemorate sailors who have died at sea. There is the small bronze plaque to the 831 Belgian merchant seamen who died in World War Two, and a memorial to U-boat hunter Captain Johnny Walker, whose tiny flotilla used to leave Liverpool to the strains of 'A-hunting we will go'. A limestone half-moon seating around a column remembers the merchant seamen who died while serving with the Royal Navy and who have no grave but the sea; plaque after plaque of names cast in bronze, folded like the pages of a book, above the quiet brown water. The British merchant sailors who died on the great convoys across the Atlantic or through the Arctic Sea to Russia are commemorated by a great bandstand and a quotation from Shakespeare's King John; 'These her Princes are come home'. On the wall beside the cut is a plaque commemorating Anglo-American sacrifice and wartime unity and a simple, powerful sculpture called *Seven Seas*, and the road in front of the Graces is called Canada Boulevard, remembering the Canadian dead with an avenue of maple trees. There is dignity in these monuments, and a quiet strength.

Over the cut that once supported the bridge down to the floating landing stage is the **Memorial to the Engine Room Heroes.** This stands in a neat landscape of paths and borders, its great carved figures staring stoically out to sea. It was originally intended as a monument to the engineers lost on the *Titanic* in 1912, but as World War One began it was decided to dedicate it to all the heroes of the engine room who had died at sea. This dignified and imposing monument was designed by William Goscombe John, who

The monument to the 'Engine Room Heroes'.

also designed the King's Regiment memorial in St John's Gardens.

From the great open memorial space of the Pier Head, we turn down **St Nicholas's Place** towards the Dock Road, here called **George's Dock Gates**, to admire the other sides of the Three Graces. The massive wall of the Royal Liver Building to our right marks roughly the end of George's Dock. All the ground beneath our feet so far on this walk has been claimed from the river; the high stone wall ahead of us in front of St Nicholas's church marks the old shoreline. This is remembered in the street name Strand, meaning a shore or beach, and in a tiny street called Sea Brow which still runs through the car park on Redcross Street.

Subtleties of street name, here as poetic and evocative as anywhere else in the city, are lost on the thousands of drivers and passengers who thunder down this road every day. This stretch of the dock road is six lanes of permanently busy traffic, which has been criticised for amputating the Pier Head and the Albert Dock from the rest of the city. But above the noise of the traffic the buildings are tall and impressive, and there is a wealth of history here. The white-tiled building

George's Dock building and the Three Graces.

opposite, for example, is Tower Building, built in 1906 by Walter Aubrey Thomas, who also designed the Royal Liver Building. It was faced in white tiles to counteract the soot and grease in the air, and had big windows to let in as much light as possible. The subtle towers on the roofline are a reference to the building that used to stand here; the

Piazza Waterfall, in the courtyard of Wilberforce House, now Beetham Plaza.

Tower of Liverpool. It was a square building on the waterfront, with small towers and a quadrangle behind, which belonged to the Stanleys of Knowsley, the Earls of Derby. Over the centuries they used it as fortress, prison, bolthole, warehouse, and departure point for their lands in the Isle of Man. It was used by the Corporation as a gaol and was as old as any structure in Liverpool, possibly as old as the Castle, but the Tower was demolished in the early 19th century.

The bridge ahead of us takes us to the courtyard of Wilberforce House, and a little square with a famous sculpture. Officially called the *Piazza Waterfall*, this is known locally as 'the Contraption'. It is a series of steel buckets on slim bronze posts, which tip with the weight of water sending gallons crashing down into the basin. It is a lovely sculpture, lively and exciting, noisy and unpredictable, and was designed in 1966 by Richard Huws. The old Wilberforce House has been renovated as expensive and exclusive apartments, and the courtyard revitalised with smart restaurants as **Beetham Plaza**.

The dock road below us is divided by a central reservation. The road heading north is called **the Goree**, and the road going south, along the old shoreline, is called the **Strand**; but it was once called Back Goree and the old roads ran either side of a warehouse complex called the Goree Piazzas. This was built in the late 18th century to

The Goree Piazzas, 1913. *(LCC)*

hold goods for George's Dock. Sometimes even Liverpool's little history is stained with the slave trade; the piazza was named after an island off Senegal used as a holding camp for slaves, which is now a World Heritage Site. The first warehouse burned down in 1802 in the biggest fire the town had ever seen, and the ruins smouldered for three months before being rebuilt. Nathaniel Hawthorne had his consular offices near here, in Washington Buildings at the lower corner of Brunswick Street, which he described as 'a shabby and smoke-stained edifice of four storeys high'. Washington Irving worked in the Goree Piazzas itself, as a merchant for a firm whose bankruptcy drove him to start writing. The Goree Piazzas these American writers knew survived until being bombed during World War Two, and was then demolished. By then the once-imposing warehouse was dwarfed by the giant buildings of the Pier Head.

A street sign naming the street as the Goree can be seen on the side of the George's Dock Building, tucked away behind the Port of Liverpool building. This is in fact a huge ventilating chimney for the first Mersey Tunnel, and has nothing to do with George's Dock apart from being built over it. It was designed by Herbert Rowse in the distinctive Art Deco style that he used for the Tunnel, and has a giant collar of offices rising five storeys from the ground. The building sits in a little piazza of its own, and for a seemingly plain building is highly decorated, from the lightning flashes suitably warning the unwary to the solemn basalt sculptures of *Night* and *Day* – commemorating the ever-open tunnel – on the George's Dock Way entrance. The sculpture was by Edmund

Goree Piazzas being cleared, showing Pier Head Station on the Overhead Railway, 1949. *(LCC)*

The solemn basalt sculpture *Night*.

Thompson, assisted by George Capstick. The most moving design faces the Goree, and remembers the men who died during the construction of the Tunnel.

Across the road from the George's Dock Building is Albion House, built as the head-quarters of the White Star Line. It was designed by Richard Norman Shaw and James Francis Doyle, and strongly resembles Shaw's New Scotland Yard building on the banks of the Thames. It was built in 1897 as 'part Loire château part Hanseatic warehouse' in Quentin Hughes's words, and is a dramatic feature of dull James Street, and a strong turning point from the Strand.

The street opposite Albion House is called **Mann Island**. It crosses what was once George's Dock Passage, a narrow canal connecting Canning Dock with George's Dock. With Manchester Dock behind, and the locks controlling the flow of water and vessels, a small man-made island was formed. The 'island' was supposedly named after John Mann, who lived on the dock estate. It was jokingly referred to as 'Mann's Island' and by

A passageway on the site of Nova Scotia, from where packet boats used to run to Dublin.

the 1790s the name was officially adopted. This reclaimed land was large enough to have two streets on it, Irwell Street and **Nova Scotia**. The Dublin packet boats ran from Nova Scotia and the offices for the shipping line were here. These narrow streets teemed with life; this was part of the 'sailor town' that ran from here to Paradise Street and they were crammed with sailors' taverns and brothels, warehouses and doss-houses, and would have smelled of rope, of salt, of old wool and sweat, tobacco, fish, and stale beer slops.

Once again, big changes are mooted for this area, 100 years after the Three Graces changed the waterfront landscape. The Leeds & Liverpool Canal will be extended from Stanley Dock across the Pier Head to the Albert Dock, and a new tramway system will once again use the Pier Head as a terminus. Most controversially, a fourth Grace has been proposed for Mann Island, a huge modern glass swirl of a building by architect Will Alsop, already nicknamed the Cloud. If they come to anything, these plans would certainly rejuvenate the Pier Head, but they are not without their opponents. Mann Island takes us back to the Pier Head and we return to the **Albert Dock**.

WALK 11
A Short Woodland Walk

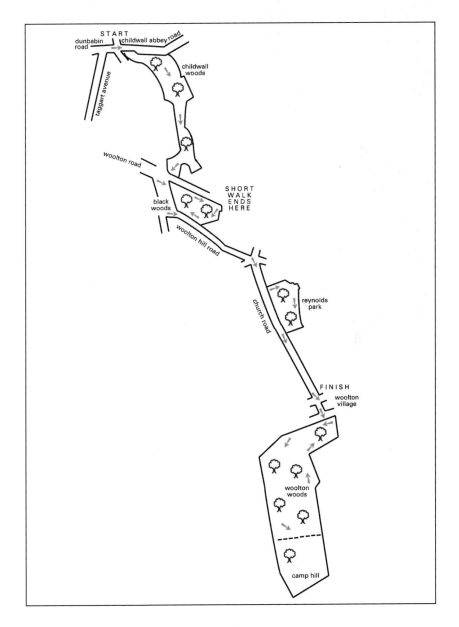

Two views of Childwall Woods.

This walk explores a stretch of parks and thick woodland in Liverpool, from Childwall Woods to Woolton. It is possible to spend an afternoon doing an exploratory loop through Childwall Woods and Black Woods, but the walk has also been extended to include Woolton and its parks and woods.

Childwall Woods was the estate surrounding Childwall Hall, and was laid out in the late 18th century when the estate was developed from the Childwall Heath, moorland that stretched as far as Wavertree and Allerton. In the 1780s the estate was owned by the Gascoyne family, and was also owned at one time by Isaac Green, the Liverpool lawyer who speculated wisely in property in the 18th and early 19th century. The Hall was demolished in 1949 and the site occupied first by Childwall College and now by Phil Redmond's Mersey TV Company.

Childwall Woods is a good place for an afternoon's ramble and picnic, and a great landscape for children to explore, as many of the features of the Hall's parkland – worn sandstone steps, the carriageway, even an artificial island – are still here, under huge rhododendron thickets, the overgrown remains of the formal planting scheme. This is more of a chance for woodland exploration and an afternoon away from traffic or buildings, than a prescribed walk. Childwall Woods is unlike other parks in the city; it is wilder than anywhere else, with the exceptions of the huge woods out in Croxteth Park or the forest wilderness of Otterspool, and generations of children have turned it into a playground, populating it with pirates and cowboys, and building dens and secret hideaways. For that reason the route is a suggestion only, and every opportunity should be taken to get off the beaten track and explore further.

The walk starts at **Taggart Avenue shops**, where **Childwall Abbey Road** leads us to the entrance to **Childwall Woods**. The neat lodge house at the entrance is possibly by the great Regency architect John Nash, as he designed Childwall Hall from 1780 onwards. It is the only surviving building on the estate.

The lodge at the entrance to Childwall Woods.

A surviving doorway near the site of Childwell Hall, possibly designed by John Nash.

Trees in the woods, 2004.

After 100 yards or so, the old carriageway to the Hall appears on our right, a well-defined walk through the woods. It can become slippery and muddy after wet weather, however, and the path to its left follows the carriageway and is dryer and better maintained. We follow the path round as it shadows the line of the carriageway.

Childwall Woods is a long and relatively narrow piece of woodland, and so it is difficult to become lost as most of the paths double back on themselves. Almost all the paths that lead off the main route through the Woods can be taken to explore it further. New clearings are opened in the dense rhododendron undergrowth as the giant forest trees fall, and new paths are made by local children and dog walkers. The giant beech trees rise above the rhododendrons and holly bushes, and open out occasionally into wide glades. Sometimes the trees and bushes make the path narrow and secret, at others we are walking on wide paths under a great canopy of leaves.

After a few minutes, a small set of sandstone steps appears on the left. These lead to a small hidden path which curves round to the right and another shallow flight of steps. The path then splits around an artificial 'island', immensely popular with local children. The island has steep cliffs and care should be taken, but the gorges on either side are interesting and both lead to the path at the far end of the island, which in turn leads to the bridge. These paths can be very muddy after rain.

The bridge is a modern replacement of a rickety wooden structure which swung alarmingly, and was replaced some years ago. Below is the carriageway, now sweeping

Root and stone, Childwall Woods.

around dramatically through the sandstone walls of its gorge to approach the Hall. The Hall was built in a heavy mediaeval style, and the whole must have presented a suitably Gothic vision to visitors.

On the other side of the carriageway is a path leading to Countisbury Drive and Childwall Park Avenue. These large houses date from the 1920s and 1930s, and have great views into the woods.

Through the trees and fence at the bottom of the hill to our left can be seen the petrol station and shops of the TV series *Brookside*, which was partly filmed here and partly filmed on the Brookside Close set in West Derby.

Take the broad path to the left, which goes between the tumbled stones of a great wall. The rhododendrons do not grow here, and the astonishing height of these mature trees can be seen. There was once the heavy gravestone of a Great Dane next to the wall, a family pet belonging to the family that once lived here and buried on their estate. With the wall's gradual disintegration the gravestone seems to have disappeared.

The stretch beyond the old wall is roughly spanner shaped, and leads us towards Woolton Road. The trees are more spaced out here, and the ground seems more spacious, more open. To our left now are the wide fields surrounding the Alice Elliot School. It is easy to forget how high the ground is here, but the field falls away quite steeply towards Childwall Lane and the view stretches away towards Huyton and Prescot church, visible on a clear day on the horizon. The fence has collapsed, but the original

Black Woods, on the other side of Woolton Road from Childwall Woods.

stones defining the 18th-century estate can be seen, together with perhaps the remains of a ha-ha preventing grazing animals from climbing into the ornamental woods. These grounds are private but have been left wild, and with small clumps of beech and birch trees and the paths through the grass, it is difficult to imagine that we are in a major city; there are no roads, no buildings on the horizon, just the sigh of the grass and the wind in the trees. We follow the path through the trees to **Woolton Road**. On the other side of the road is **Black Woods**, a compact patch of dense beech woodland. In autumn the trees are a rich bronze colour, and the woods are refreshingly free of rhododendrons.

The old carriageway through Childwall Woods.

Boundary wall of the old Childwall Hall Estate.

Crossing **Woolton Road** we turn down **Aldbourne Avenue**. The entrance to **Black Woods** is through a gate immediately on our right at the very beginning of the road. The paths here are even easier to follow than those in Childwall Woods; take the path to left or right and it will lead you around the Woods, which are not very extensive. Some of the beech trees here are very old, with some real forest giants in clearings in the middle of the woods. Black Woods is not big, but it is very dense, and in spring and summer the beech foliage is very thick. The surrounding roads disappear very quickly, and the only sound is birdsong, incredible in a small wood near a main road. There are a number of paths across the middle of the woodland, which will bring you out sooner or later on the broad path on the outside. Follow the paths through the woods or walk the circumferential path around to your entrance point.

Crossing Woolton Road again, we retrace our steps through **Childwall Woods** – perhaps by a different route as all will broadly lead us to the main entrance – to **Taggart Avenue**. There are shops and a restaurant on the triangle at Taggart Avenue, and to the right as we leave Childwall Woods is the old village of Childwall. All that survives today is the sandstone church of All Saints, dating back to the Middle Ages, and the Childwall Abbey Hotel. This is another very old building and today has something of the Gothic Revival atmosphere that Childwall Hall must once have had, with dark panelling and heavy furniture. It used to have the only quoits pitch in Liverpool, and serves good food and beer.

For a longer ramble, continue the walk from Black Woods. Instead of retracing our steps, we leave Black Woods at the gate onto **Woolton Hill**, at the end of **Aldbourne Avenue**. This area was large estates surrounding country houses until the 1920s and 1930s, when many of the present houses were built. The long sandstone walls and lodge houses from these estates have often survived, and in some cases the country houses themselves have been retained as private schools or offices. Today this is a quiet residential district. There were once many quarries in this area providing the stone for buildings and boundaries, and many of the walls on Woolton Hill are made of the local sandstone. The biggest and most famous of these old workings is Woolton Quarry in the village. It is now closed and has modern houses built on it, but the great walls of the quarry can still be seen.

Woolton Hill takes us to the roundabout at the top of **Blackwood Avenue**, with a fine avenue of mature trees dropping down to Woolton Road. At the bottom is a further fragment of mature woodland. We are now on the crest of Woolton Hill, and on a clear day there are good views from here towards Prescot and Huyton. The other roads here are equally interesting. Beaconsfield Road has Strawberry Field on it, the Salvation Army home visited by the young John Lennon, and Woolton Hill Road opposite leads across Rose Brow to the urban village of Gateacre, with its pretty cottages and well-preserved village green.

Church Road to our right leads us after 100 yards or so to **Reynolds Park**. This is one of the most curious of Liverpool's parks, secretive and strangely shaped. The old house which stood here was demolished not long ago, but some curious details of the grounds have survived; steps to empty platforms, sandstone shelters, and paths that seem to go nowhere. One of the sadder stories about John Lennon in Woolton is of him coming here with his then girlfriend not long after his mother died, and ranting and raving in his grief

Reynolds Park, 2004.

The sundial walk, Reynolds Park.

The sunken garden at Camp Hill.

and anger at the injustice of her death. The park has some immense trees, good views across Childwall Valley, and some interesting nooks and crannies, including the walled garden, which is very beautiful during the summer months and one of the most magical hidden gardens of the city.

Church Road leads us past the fine Gothic St Peter's church, where once Paul McCartney sang in the choir, to Woolton village. Woolton deserves an afternoon's exploring on its own, as it has many attractive buildings, shops, pubs and restaurants, and seems surrounded by the green spaces of Allerton Golf Course and Woolton Woods.

The walk ends in Woolton, but can be extended for a ramble through Woolton Woods and Camp Hill, which form one of the great open spaces of south Liverpool, a great place for a picnic and for children to explore. The Hill is one of the knuckles of stone on the great spine of sandstone that follows the river from here to Everton. It was supposedly settled a century and a half before the Roman invasion, but nothing remains today of the Iron Age village. The crown of the hill has great tall beech trees, and thick holly bushes, and on the far side there are superb views over Speke and the river, across the Wirral to the Welsh hills.

Houses in Woolton village, at the end of the walk.

Woolton village has cafés and restaurants and many good pubs that serve food. The White Horse is especially attractive, the Elephant is bustly and cheerful, and the Grapes and the Coffee House are more traditional Liverpool pubs. The main road through the village has buses into Liverpool city centre, and the 173 bus service runs from outside the Village Hall to Taggart Avenue where the walk began, although this service only runs until six o'clock in the evening.

WALK 12

Frenzied Poets and Sober Men

An Architectural Pub Crawl

'The city, as I remember it then, seemed garishly bright and noisy...'
Rupert Croft-Cooke, essay on Liverpool.

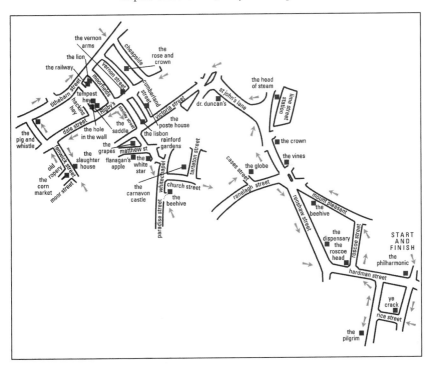

This is a walk arranged to connect a very personal chain of pubs. Everyone who drinks in the city will have favourite and least favourite pubs, and this walk links my choice of pubs that are curious, odd, architecturally appealing, or just off the beaten track. Some also serve good beer or do food, and some do neither.

Liverpool is a drinking city, and its social life revolves around the pub. The city's pubs are where evenings start and end, lunch meetings happen, reports are written. They have live music, poetry readings or theatre performances in the evenings, and during the day serve as offices, debating chambers, and cafés. Trade happens here too, and the variety of goods you could be offered is astonishing – rag mags, tobacco, cockles, leather jackets.

There are back-street dives with rough wooden floors, tiny dapper corner pubs of polished brass and mosaic, opulent Victorian rooms of marble and heavy shiny tile, and huge *fin-de-siècle* gin palaces reeking of cigar smoke and Edwardian decadence. The drinkers are as diverse as the pubs, and you can meet artists and students, fat and red-faced businessmen, cheery girls drinking in pairs or huge gangs, gentle lifelong boozers with cracked faces, bar-room philosophers, dapper ex-boxers, poets, street watchers. The sailors and the prostitutes have largely gone, but otherwise all of old Liverpool life is here. The pubs open in time for lunch and are open all day, but some in the city centre – especially in the commercial district – are not open after about 9pm, as all their business takes place during the day.

The history of Liverpool's pubs is thoroughly explored in Freddy O'Connor's excellent series *A Pub On Every Corner*.

The walk starts at the **Philharmonic Hotel** on Hope Street, built between 1898 and 1900. This is the most famous of the city's pubs, renowned for its fantastic Art Nouveau décor and marble toilets. The main bar has great sweeps of mosaic, stained-glass windows, and beaten copper panelling. There is a roaring fire in the winter. The smaller rooms – Brahms and Liszt, of course – are darker and more intimate, but still have wainscoting, stained glass, and fine fireplaces. The large room at the end used to have jazz and blues gigs, and is now used for pub food, and there are more formal dining rooms upstairs. The Phil is popular with students and still, perhaps, the musicians from the other Phil across the road.

From the Philharmonic we turn right along Hope Street, past the Philharmonic Hall to Rice Street. The old warehouses here have gone, and the only old building is **Ye Cracke**, built out of two 18th-century houses. This is the city's most bohemian pub, with wooden floors and fine beer. Art students drink here, and it is famous for its links with the Beatles, as John Lennon and Stu Sutcliffe were at Art School just around the corner. It also has the tiny War Room, supposedly where drinkers met to discuss the progress of the Boer War. In the summer the Cracke has a fine beer garden at the back, one of the few decent places in the city to drink outdoors.

Students from the Art School and the Liverpool Institute of the Performing Arts also drink and eat in **the Pilgrim**, down Rice Street on Pilgrim Street. This busy pub is almost entirely underground, with huge (and not very good) paintings of the Beatles over the tables. It is a curiously successful mixture of a Bavarian beer hall and an American milk bar from the 1950s. The main body of the room is wooden, with heavy beams, a resounding wooden floor and a long wooden table down the middle, and the side walls are divided into tiny alcoves with tiny jukeboxes on the walls, all red panels with stars and steel, and a genuine fold back method of reading the track lists. The Pilgrim is renowned for large portions of simple pub food, and it too has more formal dining rooms upstairs.

Behind the Post Office on Leece Street is **the Roscoe Head**, an older and less 'studenty' pub. It is housed in a simple Georgian building on Roscoe Street, and both are named after William Roscoe, writer, anti-slavery campaigner, and cultural giant. Known affectionately as the little Roscoe, the pub has tiny rooms, excellent beer, and good food. The small rooms encourage conversation, and the clientele are often university staff, quieter students or businessmen. Under a previous landlord the Roscoe Head was known for its collection of ties, which hung, knotted or folded, around the picture rail and shelf of the main room. It is a typical Liverpool pub, well maintained and well run,

The Beehive on Mount Pleasant.

and all the city's pubs should be like this.

Walking along Roscoe Street, we turn left onto Mount Pleasant and walk down the hill. **The Beehive** on Mount Pleasant is a fine Victorian pub with an amazing high ceiling and rich plaster carving. Postmen drink in here from the nearby Copperas Hill sorting office, and sometimes railway staff from Lime Street Station. There is also a hard core of polite older drinkers, men with greased quiffs and old-fashioned suits, older women jiving and bopping like they were sweet 16, and out to dance all afternoon. Perhaps because of them the Beehive has an excellent jukebox (but not much after 1957), and an air of old-world courtesy. It seems to belong in the north end of the city rather than the city centre.

The Vines, or the Big House, is another of the city's famous pubs. It stands on Lime Street, opposite the Adelphi, and is a riot of Edwardian exuberance. Inside the pub has deep, heavy plasterwork and gilding, fine beaten copper panels, and a gigantic dining room that used to have large oil paintings hanging from the walls. This is big enough to be used for dances on occasion. The pub's useless, top-heavy tower and heavy stonework make it a landmark on Lime Street, which used to have many drinking places, and the Vines has kept an air of old-fashioned seediness.

On the other end of the city block from the Vines is the **Crown**, another flamboyant gin palace which has retained its architectural splendour since 1905. It has wide rooms, a long bar, and serves good food, but the most amazing thing about it is the ceiling. It seems about three feet above your head, because it is so deep and ornate and richly

The Vines, on Lime Street.

The Crown, another flamboyant gin palace.

painted. There are cut-glass windows, hammered copper panels, and rich dark woodwork, but for all its magnificence the Crown has an air of sedate madness.

We can cut through the railway station to the **Head of Steam**, a pub carved out of the derelict North Western Hotel a few years ago. It has one good bar, the long room facing Lord Nelson Street, which Alfred Waterhouse originally intended to be a great open porch for taxi-cabs to drop off and pick up. The conversion makes the most of the pretty Gothic detailing, and the spectacular dimensions of the building. The bar next door has walls of railway memorabilia, but the other rooms have been trampled into theme rooms, although all seem to have the giant columns of the old station dining rooms rising through them. The convenient cut-through from the station concourse is sometimes closed, but here are displayed Waterhouse's original plans for the building, perhaps the one place in the city that his signature is on public display. The convenience for the platforms means that the long room has the feel of an old station bar to it, a 1940s Graham Greene sort of world full of mackintoshed salesmen consulting timetables and maps and marooned travellers between trains, whiling away the time. The Head of Steam serves good beer, and has excellent and unusual views of St George's Hall.

Alfred Waterhouse also designed **Doctor Duncan's** on St John's Lane, but this building was originally the entrance hall for the Pearl Assurance Company.

The Head of Steam, which has the
atmosphere of an old station bar.

Doctor Duncan's, also designed by Alfred Waterhouse.

Waterhouse gave the Pearl a dazzling room like an Oriental baths, huge columns and vaulting, acres of tiling and mosaic. The quieter room which wraps around this astonishing room is sedate by comparison, but nonetheless resembles a waiting room on the Indian Railway, all deep blue walls and greased brass, with old Cain's advertising posters and Victorian medical pages like warnings against the local food. In the winter the boots of urban explorers are stretched to the fire, comparing street names, maps and pretty girls over plates of chips and good strong beer. Doctor Duncan's is one of the few pubs that appeals to drinkers of all ages, and rowdy businessmen drink alongside quiet students.

The Vernon on Dale Street serves very good food and has one of the best slopes of any pub in the city centre. It is a real ale pub and the beer is always interesting. It has high ceilings of heavy plaster, and a more private room at the back, of heavy benches and partitions. The city clerks and pinstriped men from Municipal Buildings now drink

The Vernon.

elsewhere, and the Vernon often entertains arts administrators and filmmakers. Further along Dale Street, **Thomas Rigby's** is supposedly the oldest pub in the city dating from 1726. It has been recently restored and serves dangerously good beer. This is a modernised old-fashioned pub, a little fake-Tudor, but softened by usage and disparaging laughter. There is a Nelson room, with memorabilia of the Admiral, whose wine merchant built an estate in Everton. The courtyard behind the pub has been refurbished and now houses a smart restaurant.

On the corner of Dale Street and Hackins Hey is **the Saddle**. Once Dale Street had many of the coaching inns of Liverpool, and the coaches began the long run to London and Manchester from the Angel Inn or the Golden Lion. The Saddle has the restless energy of the coaching days about it; old White Star bills and letters on the

Inside the Vernon.

Gargoyles on Rigby's building.

The Saddle, on the corner of
Dale Street and Hackins Hey.

walls, underground toilets; it
seems to be a waiting room,
and everybody seems to be on
the way to somewhere else.
But it serves a good pint and
sandwiches, and the huge
windows make it an excellent
point from which to watch the
light slowly move across the
Royal Insurance building.

The Hole in the Wall on
Hackins Hey used to be the
only pub in the city with an
upstairs cellar; the beer was
gravity fed from barrels over
the bar. It has been recently

The Hole in the Wall. It used to
be the only pub in the city with
an upstairs cellar.

refurbished and its fine panelled walls cleaned, and it once again attracts a mixed crowd of businessmen and drinkers.

The Slaughterhouse on Fenwick Street is a modern Irish pub serving creamy Guinness and big lunches. The story goes that it was once a slaughterhouse, with the big hooks in the ceiling used for hauling carcasses from the floor for gutting. The beams and hooks are still there, as is the solid stone floor. The Slaughterhouse is popular with chatty office girls or mixed groups of clerks and typists, who talk business and office gossip. It has recently been refurbished and opened up, and it now looks as it did 30 years ago.

Hidden away on the other side of Fenwick Street is **the Cornmarket**. It sits between two of the town's old ropewalks, Moor Street and narrow, truncated Old Ropery and is one of the secrets of Liverpool, with a dull 1960s concrete exterior hiding a rich interior of deep red carpets, and old wall lights reflected in polished brass. Above all it has a room of Jacobean panelling, rich wainscoting and a very ornate fireplace, with deep Chesterfield armchairs and settees, a room from a gentlemen's club or a dismantled baronial castle.

From the Cornmarket it is a five-minute walk to **the Pig & Whistle** on the corner of Covent Garden and Chapel Street, a survivor from the 18th century, possibly the oldest building on the street. It is overshadowed by the giant office blocks surrounding it, and lost the rest of its block during the Blitz. Famously the pub provided food for long sea voyages during the 19th century, and the worn sign Emigrants Supplied hangs in the bar. The Pig & Whistle still has little rooms and tiny bars, and is a pub of real character.

On Tithebarn Street, the continuation of Chapel Street, stand **the Railway** and **the Lion**. The Railway is a large confident Italianate pub, with big grand rooms and a long bar. It is a good pub for a function, and seems to have more and bigger rooms at the back; named after the railway

The etched glass of the Railway, reflecting the tower of St Nicholas's Church.

Two views of the Lion, on the corner of Moorfields.

station opposite it seems a good place to find lost travellers or people waiting for a train, although the trains left Exchange for good in 1977. The Lion, at the end of the block on the corner of Moorfields, is altogether cosier; there are strong mosaics, rich tiling and a glass cupola with a giant lamp. The bar is solidly wooden and divided by cut-glass panels, as bars should be. Tithebarn Street has other pubs, remnants of the street's Italianate façades, mostly recently renovated to appeal to the John Moores students who now drink up here. The Brunswick Bar has dark wooden booths, heavy velvet curtains, and serves good beer. The Rising Sun has fared less well, and has been spit-and-sawdusted to old Ireland, where the banter never stops flowing. Across the road on the corner of Cheapside is the shell of the United Powers, commemorating wartime alliances with the United States, and one of the older buildings on the street. It was spectacularly blown up recently for a television film, and is currently boarded solid, its giant bar smoke-blackened and silent.

Cheapside has the tiny **Rose & Crown** pub, which serves big plain pub lunches from its tiny kitchen. It is immediately opposite the city's main Bridewell, and used to be full of policemen at lunchtime before such things were frowned upon. For that reason it was affectionately known as the Pig and Whistle.

Crossing Dale Street we come to Cumberland Street and **the Poste House**, a tiny old-fashioned pub recently saved from demolition. It has preserved the atmosphere of a chop house or an oyster bar from the 1870s, full of red-faced businessmen and delicate shop girls. It has hard leather benches and a tiny upstairs bar, tiled walls and a city centre clientele of office workers and city councillors, through which the staff swerve unerringly with plates of food.

On the corner of Stanley Street and Victoria Street is a little gay enclave. There are a gay bar or two on Stanley Street, and the magnificent **Lisbon** on the corner. It would be more accurate to say under the corner, since the pub is completely below ground level. The ceiling is astonishing, with heavy decoration and extravagant plasterwork. There seems to be much fancy engraved and painted mirror work, usually associated with Victorian pubs but here happily reminiscent of a delicate Wildean flamboyance. It is part of a superbly decorative building, with ornate iron grilles and elaborate windows right up to the roofline. The old post office opposite has yet more heavy decoration and weather-beaten cherubs, who seem to look wistfully across at the Lisbon.

Crossing Victoria Street and cutting down Temple Court, we come to **the Grapes** on Mathew Street. This is the sort of pub Dylan Thomas drank in to hear stories. It is a Carmarthen pub mysteriously uprooted to busy Mathew Street, a market day pub, all high back pews and scrubbed table tops. It should be full of fat tweedy farmers talking about cattle prices, but instead there are distant memories of the Beatles. A recent renovation of this pub revealed an earlier history, old wallpaper that served as a backdrop for photographs of the juvenile Beatles, a tiny scrap of wall that is forever 1961, but which now seems to have been removed in yet another facelift.

Flanagan's Apple opposite is a modern Irish pub. This warehouse has had many lives, from the old fruit and vegetable days to the 1970s when it was home to imaginative

The Grapes on Mathew Street.

urban redevelopment pioneers including the famous Armadillo Tea Rooms, with its clouds of steam and thousand teas. Outside is a bust of Carl Jung, and his famous quotation 'Liverpool is the Pool of Life'. The pub has thick brick walls and heavy iron doors, and feels like a fortress, a good place to watch the life on Mathew Street if you can get a seat by the windows. It serves thick Guinness and has huge tables, with butchers' bikes and flat irons hanging from the rafters; it is a busy, bombed-out smoky-shaft-of-sunlight sort of pub, with live music in the dripping cellar downstairs, and an edgy, excited atmosphere, like the Black and Tans have just left – or are just arriving.

Mathew Street becomes Rainford Gardens, and on the right is another of the best pubs in

Flanagan's Apple, the first modern Irish pub in the city.

Liverpool. **The White Star** is an old-fashioned back street boozer, refurbished but never surgically altered, a refuge from street noises and shopping, renowned for the quality of its Bass beer. Worlds collide in the White Star. Grizzled men in training shoes and football shirts bring their grandchildren here to watch the football, and during international championships the ceiling is hung with strips of flags, perhaps a legacy of the pub's many twin taverns. Yet it also has the strange distance of old theatre posters and luggage labels from great liners; Shanghai, New York, Hamburg, echoes of the Beatles discovering whisky and nightclubs. It is a dignified pub, traditional on many levels. The seafood men still visit the White Star, selling prawns and crabsticks; the tobacco man, with his pouches of rolly tobacco, but the pub is also visited by all manner of edgy scallies with shirts, socks, ties and watches. Not that long ago, gently retired men used to sip the Bass and play chess here, and there are plenty of mackintoshes still hung up at lunchtime and the newspapers read. There used to be men who had drunk in the White Star for 40 years who had never once set foot in the back room.

It is now possible to walk onto Whitechapel through the Wetherspoon's pub called the Welkin. This tasteful adaptation of a derelict space has floor to ceiling glass windows, which allow spectacular views of the sunlight on the faces of the old warehouses on Rainford Gardens and Button Street. It is a shame that Philip, Son & Nephew, the Liverpool booksellers, had to go from this space, as the views from the very top floor were unrivalled; a Dickensian view of wobbly chimney pots and slate roofs, old brick walls and sunlight through dusty windows into empty offices. The very top floor sold rubbers and nibs for fountain pens and was a place of pilgrimage for generations of would-be writers.

Crossing the bustle of Whitechapel, there is a tiny pub on the left hand side of Paradise Street called **the Beehive**, known as 'the Beehive on Paradise Street' to distinguish it from the one on Mount Pleasant. This long thin pub, with its one vast traditional pub window, has walls of old books and displays of shells arranged in circles

Tiles in the White Star pub.

The Beehive on
Paradise Street.

and lines like old pikes and swords in Scottish castles. It used to have big comfy couches and hard stools, if you could get a seat; this pub always seems full of people. There has been a restaurant here since before World War One and there are photographs showing the pub in 1914, its ornate interior recognisable today. It is a convenient place for men to be tethered safely while their wives go shopping, and is popular with the local market traders, who appreciate the good mixed grills. The Beehive is thick with cigarette smoke and the smell of tomatoes frying, and used to have a free juke box pumping out Billy J. Kramer and Roy Orbison.

The Carnarvon Castle, on Tarleton Street off Church Street, is a grandmother's parlour writ large; lace curtains and gentle winter fires, horse brasses, stained glass, and thick cheese sandwiches. It used to be famous for its collection of valuable Dinky toys, and its glass cases are still full of interesting and unusual objects. It is a good pub to watch people in and from, an escape-from-the-rain-sort of pub, on the concrete canyon of Tarleton Street. Shoppers drink here surrounded by bags of bargains, before catching an unsteady bus home.

Through modern Clayton Square is the tiny **Globe**, on Cases Street. Once most pubs in the city centre were like this, noisy lively places; the fruit and vegetable barrows outside retain the bustle of a market street long gone from the rest of the city centre. It is an old-fashioned pub, a crowded, polite, friendly place full of old people sat for the afternoon after some shopping, and people called in for a swift half and not even sitting down; it is an ex-boxer's pub, full of dapper men in their 60s and 70s drinking halves with their wives, a quiet pub that always seems busy, and it has one of the best slopes in the city, an incline to rival the Vernon's. It also has one of the longest classical quotations in the city, possibly from Horace, that the title of this walk is taken from.

From Cases Street we turn left onto Ranelagh Street and right at the Adelphi onto Renshaw Street. Near the junction with Leece Street is **the Dispensary**. This is a modern pub in an old pub's shell; the Dispensary used to be the Grapes, which had become rundown, and perhaps a better metaphor for the city's regeneration could not be found. It is run by the city's Cain's brewery, and serves excellent ale and food. The early Victorian architecture has been treated with respect and this cheerful friendly pub looks as if it has always looked the way it does now; the creak of floorboards, the rub of old wooden chairs and tables, the gleam of polished metalwork and engraved glass.

Little cobbled Oldham Street behind the pub, currently being regenerated after decades of dereliction, takes us to Roscoe Street and a right turn onto Leece Street. **The Philharmonic**, where we began the walk, is at the top of the hill.

The Dispensary.